Roman Mili
Clothing (1)

100 BC–AD 200

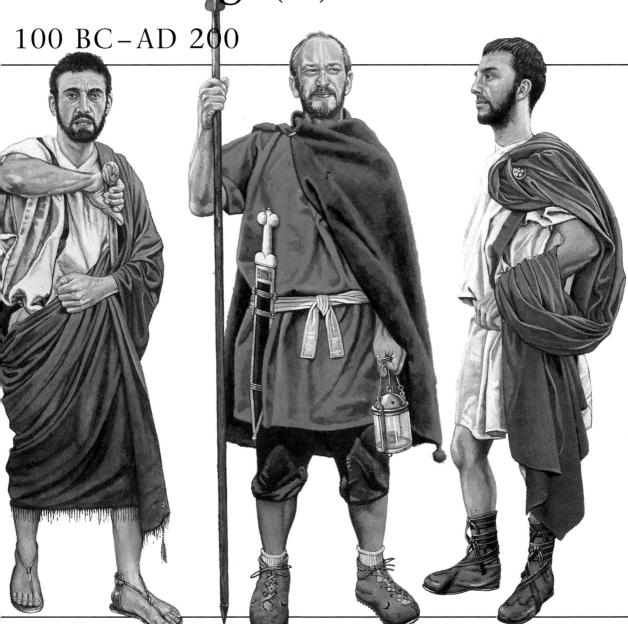

Graham Sumner

Series editor Martin Windrow

First published in Great Britain in 2002 by Osprey Publishing,
Elms Court, Chapel Way, Botley, Oxford OX2 9LP, United Kingdom.
Email: **info@ospreypublishing.com**

ISBN 1 84176 487 6

Editor: Martin Windrow
Design: Alan Hamp
Index by Alan Rutter
Originated by Magnet Harlequin, Uxbridge, UK.
Printed in China through World Print Ltd.

FOR A CATALOGUE OF ALL BOOKS PUBLISHED BY
OSPREY MILITARY AND AVIATION PLEASE CONTACT:

The Marketing Manager, Osprey Direct UK, PO Box 140
Wellingborough, Northants, NN8 2FA, United Kingdom
Email: **info@ospreydirect.co.uk**

The Marketing Manager, Osprey Direct USA,
c/o MBI Publishing, 729 Prospect Avenue, Osceola, WI 54020, USA
Email: **info@ospreydirectusa.com**

www.ospreypublishing.com

Dedication

This book is dedicated to Chris Haines and all the past and present
men and women of the Ermine Street Guard, in recognition of their
achievements in Roman research and re-enactment since the
foundation of the society in 1972.

Acknowledgements

I should like to thank Chris Haines, Clive Constable, Tony Segalini
and Martin White of the Ermine Street Guard, who all found the time
to comment on earlier versions of this text or helped with
photographs. In addition I would like to thank Mike Bishop, Carol
van Driel-Murray, Simon James, Lise Bender Jorgensen, Penelope
Rogers and especially John Peter Wild for their helpful advice and
suggestions, many of which found their way into the final text –
though any errors which remain are entirely the author's. I am
grateful to Claudio Antonucci, Massimo Bizzarri, Raffaele D'Amato
and in particular to Paul Holder, who found most of the obscure
photographs and references. I am also grateful to the following
individuals and institutions, who kindly assisted with the supply of
photographic material: Fratelli Alinari, Firenze, Italy; Alan Jeffrey
Spencer, Tania Watkins and Derek Welsby, The British Museum;
Dr Ursula Heimburg and Anita Rieche, Rheinisches Landesmuseum
Bonn; Andrew Batt, Museum of London; Malcolm Chapman, The
Manchester Museum; Charles Kline and Dr Jennifer Houser Wegner
University of Pennsylvania Museum; Robin and Pat Birley, The
Vindolanda Museum. Finally I would like to thank Andy Bodley,
Elaine Norbury and Martin Windrow, who all helped to make this
project possible.

Artist's Note

Readers may care to note that the original paintings from which the
colour plates in this book were prepared are available for private
sale. All reproduction copyright whatsoever is retained by the
Publishers. All enquiries should be addressed to:

GRAHAMKEVAN@sumner9.freeserve.co.uk

The Publishers regret that they can enter into no correspondence
upon this matter.

ROMAN MILITARY CLOTHING (1) FROM CAESAR TO COMMODUS, 100 BC – AD 200

INTRODUCTION

A soldier need not be feared if he is clothed, armed, shod, sated and has something in his money belt. (SHA, Severus Alexander, 52)

ALTHOUGH A GREAT DEAL OF ATTENTION has been paid to the armour and equipment used by the Roman Army, by comparison the basic clothing worn by the soldiers has been practically ignored. For many military historians textiles lack the glamour and appeal of armour and weapons; but it should not be forgotten that the average Roman soldier – like his modern counterpart – spent far more of his service life in everyday dress or 'fatigues' than he did in 'battledress'. Soldiers off duty and out of armour were still instantly recognisable when compared to the civilian population – a distinction which soldiers were apparently keen to stress.

The development of Roman re-enactment societies since 1972 has stimulated both a general interest in Roman clothing and textiles, and a greater appreciation amongst academics of the value of practical reconstructions. Nevertheless, the fact remains that many well preserved items of military clothing probably remain unrecognised or, worse, forgotten. As current excavations, especially in Egypt, yield still more examples of textiles, some of which could be military, there is an even greater need for this body of evidence to be studied, classified and recognised for its true value.

This study owes much to the pioneering work of Nick Fuentes, whose article 'The Roman Military Tunic', published in 1987, is the only readily available scholarly work on this subject in English. However, Fuentes himself admitted that his investigation was not exhaustive; and in the 15 years since its publication new discoveries and reports have been published, in particular from the excavations at Masada in Israel, Vindolanda and Carlisle in England, and other sites including Antinoe in Egypt and Carnuntum in Austria. These excavations have not only added to the corpus of textile finds, but have provided further clues to the colour of military clothing and the terminology originally used to describe them.

TUNICS *(TUNICA)*

There is very little evidence for the type of tunic used by the Roman army during the Republic, and reconstruction relies on a combination of literary and artistic evidence. Well-known sculptures including the Altar of Domitius Ahenobarbus and the Aemilius Paullus monument, while

Annaius Daverzus, an auxiliary soldier with Cohors IIII Delmatarum, from his gravestone found at Bingen, Germany – see Plate B2. This best preserved example of the Rhineland tombstones shows the strikingly curved drapery of the early Imperial tunic (and also a legionary-style shield). A rectangular object seems to be tucked into a waistband under his weapons belt. The fourth cohort of Dalmatians were later stationed at Hardknott Fort guarding the crest of a bleak pass in Cumbria, north west England.

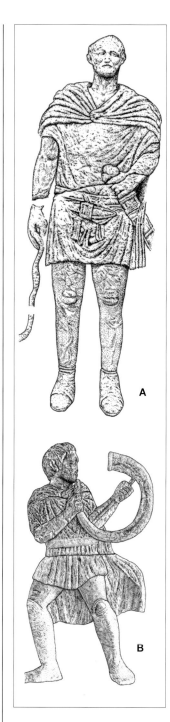

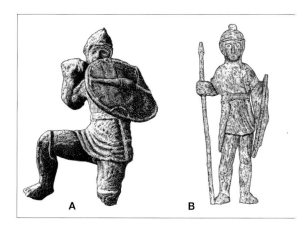

Late Republican/early Imperial tunics on bronze statuettes from Italy:
(A) Telamon,
(B) Villa Giulia, Rome. Both wear short, short-sleeved tunics.

influential on modern perceptions of Republican armour and equipment, reveal little of the tunics worn underneath.

This in itself might be thought significant, as it confirms the Roman writer Gellius (*Noct. Act.*, VI, xii, 3), who said that early Roman tunics were sleeveless and that the Romans considered long-sleeved tunics ridiculous (see also *Vir., Aen.* IX, 615). As a youth Julius Caesar was criticised for wearing a tunic with long fringed sleeves (Suet., *Caes.*, XLV). Statuettes from Telamon and the Villa Giulia, Rome, suggest little difference between late Republican and early Imperial styles. Quintilianus (*Inst. Orat.*, XI, 138) noted that when a tunic was worn above the knee it was the dress of a centurion, but from sculptural evidence it is clear that this style was also worn by 'other ranks'.

One minor punishment was that a soldier could be made to stand around the camp in an un-belted tunic, thus depriving the offender of his military appearance. We are told by Frontinus (*Strat.*, IV, I. 26) that a cohort commander named Gaius Titius, who had retreated before an army of slaves, had to endure this form of humiliation. A variation on this punishment was introduced by the Emperor Julian (AD 361–363): when a squadron of cavalry broke ranks and fled during the battle of Strasbourg, the offenders were dressed in women's clothing (Zozimus, HN. 3.3. 4–5). A similar fate befell the military martyrs Sergius and Bacchus: accused of being Christians (BHL 7599), they were stripped of their cloaks and other military garments and forced to parade in female dress. On the other hand, clothing could be handed out as a form of reward, and captured clothing was often thought worthy booty to be dedicated to the gods.

The bulk of the sculptural evidence for military clothing comes from the early Empire, more specifically between the reigns of the Emperors Tiberius (AD 14–37) and Hadrian (AD 117–138). Romans, both civilian and military, seem to have used a simple tunic which during the early Imperial period was normally quite wide and sleeveless, and some tunics appear to have been scaled up or down proportionally from a basic design. Roman tunic manufacture was entirely practical; they were simply constructed from two rectangular pieces of material sewn together and closed with seams under the arms and down the sides. Both the neck and lower openings were selvedges, which therefore made hemming unnecessary. The examples of complete tunics that survive from Israel and Egypt suggest that Fuentes was incorrect in suggesting

Late Republican/early Imperial tunics worn by soldiers from the time of Julius Caesar:
(A) Minutius, a centurion with Legio III Martia from Padua, Italy;
(B) a *cornicen* from Osuna, Seville, Spain.

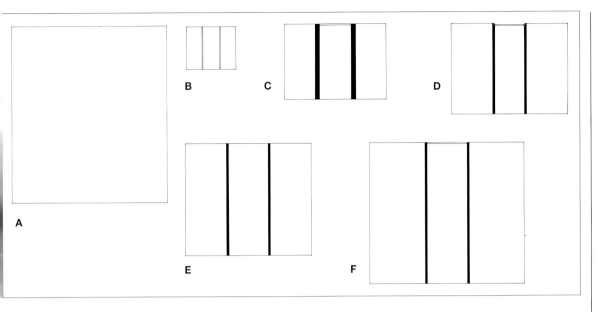

B

C

D

A

E

F

Tunic dimensions, to constant scale: (A) Military tunic description from BGU 1564 – 1.55m long x 1.40m wide. (B) Child's linen shirt, Nahal Hever, Israel, no.65-762 (after Yadin) – 0.38m long x 0.45m wide. (C) Young adult's tunic, Nahal Hever no.6-210 (after Yadin) – 0.65m long x 0.90m wide. (D) Mons Claudianus, Egypt, tunic A (after Mannering) – 0.80m long x 1.07m wide. (E) Nahal Hever, no.22-8-4 (after Yadin) – 1.0m long x 1.15m wide. (F) Nubia, Egypt, Grave Q150 (after Thurman & Williams) – 1.27m long x 1.40m wide.

Part of a rare glass vessel from Vindolanda, England, showing a gladiatorial scene. The referee in the centre wears a typical broad, sleeveless Roman tunic in a buff colour, with reddish-brown *clavi*, the two vertical stripes from shoulder to lower edge; the term came from clavus, '*nail*'. (Vindolanda Museum)

that the Roman tunic was narrow. Even as late as the 7th century AD, Maurikios (*Strat* 1.2) still described military tunics as broad and full.

However, even if the garments are complete, apart from the very small examples obviously intended for children it is almost impossible to ascertain the original owners' size, build, or even at times their sex. There is no obvious evidence that late military tunics were any smaller than in earlier periods to accommodate the reduced height requirements attested by Vegetius (*Epit.*, 1.5). The only certain estimate we have for a military tunic of any period is provided by BGU 1564, a papyrus copy from Egypt of an order for clothing and a blanket to be provided for the army in Cappadocia by the weavers of Philadelphia, which dates from around AD 138.

One tunic is specified in this document and was to be 3½ cubits long (1.55m) and 3 cubits and 4 fingers wide (1.40m) weighing 3¾ minae (1.6kg), and costing 24 drachmae. Its size is comparable with one of the largest tunics found at Nahal Hever, Israel, and it is the same width as a tunic from Nubia; but it is also interesting to note that it would have been longer than any of the examples from Nahal Hever and most other examples found elsewhere. It would also have been much longer than those recommended for farm workers by Cato (*de Agric.*, LIX), who states that they should be P.III S (1.07m) long.

Papyrus BGU 1564 specifies that all the garments should be made 'from fine soft white wool without dirt', 'well edged, pleasing and undamaged'. The fact that most military garments would have been made from wool is supported by sculptural

5

representations of tunics which show the edging methods employed for wool garments rather than for linen ones.

Many surviving tunics, including examples from Egypt and the woman's tunic from Les Martres-de-Veyre in France, had been shortened by their owners with tucks around the waist; it is therefore possible that the military tunic from Philadelphia would have needed altering in this manner. The

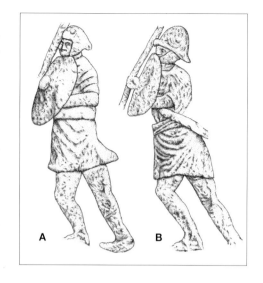

writer Tertullian (*de Pallio*, V) comments that tunics should have been made shorter in the first place to avoid the need to gather up all the loose material. It may have been considered unsightly to show these tucks around the waist, and one method of concealment could have been by a sash-like waistband.

It is not clear if military garments were produced in a variety of sizes. Cloaks probably were not, and modern re-enactors find that one standard size is suitable. However, Egyptian documents such as Columbia Papyri IX have the ambiguous Greek adjectives *teleios* and *paratelios* associated with tunics, which may describe either different types, sizes or qualities.

ABOVE **A relief from Metz, France, possibly showing a merchant and his customer examining a tunic. Although this is not a military tunic, and is probably of a type known today as a 'Gallic coat', it gives an impression of the width of contemporary Roman garments.**

ABOVE LEFT **Late Republican and early Imperial tunics – soldiers from the arch at Susa, Italy, dating from the reign of Augustus. (A) appears to be wearing a *'lorica segmentata'*, perhaps the earliest representation of this type of armour. (B) seems to wearing only a tunic with a fabric waistband.**

Costs and materials

The cost of 25 drachmae (6.25 denarii) paid to the weavers of Philadelphia in AD 138 for the military tunic can be compared with the deductions on soldiers' pay receipts for clothing in P.Geneva Lat.1. from Egypt in AD 81, and the receipt of C.Messius from Masada dated to AD 72. In the Geneva papyrus Q.Iulius Proclus had 205.5 drachmae deducted in one year towards clothing, while his comrade C.Valerius Germanus was docked 245.5 drachmae (61.375 denarii). In the last pay period they had 60 drachmae (15 denarii) and 100 drachmae (25 denarii) deducted respectively, which can be contrasted with the 7 denarii (equivalent to 28 drachmae) paid for a linen tunic by C.Messius.

The effects of the economic, military and political crisis which befell the empire from the late 2nd century onwards can be seen in the hugely inflated cost of clothing as illustrated by the price edict issued in AD 301 during the reign of the Emperor Diocletian (AD 284–305). Here we find that there are three grades of military tunic available, costing respectively 1,000, 1,250 and 1,500 denarii.

In Republican times the Greek historian Polybius records how deductions were made from Roman soldiers' pay for food and clothing. Later, according to Plutarch (*C.Gracchus*, V), one of the reforms introduced by the Tribune C.Gracchus was that soldiers should be supplied with clothing at the public expense. However, it is well known that soldiers in the early Principate once again had money deducted to

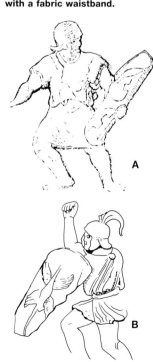

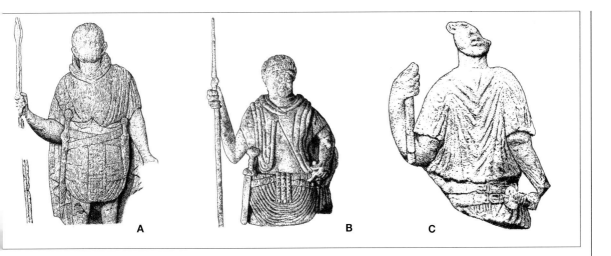

A   B   C

Early Imperial tunics showing drapery effects on tombstones soldiers from the Rhineland area of Germany:
(A) Firmus, of the Cohors Raetorum, from Andernach, and
(B) unidentified, from Bonn – both wearing *paenula* cloaks;
(C) unidentified, from Bingen.

pay for their equipment, and documents like those above show that clothing was amongst the most expensive of these items, with around 30 per cent of a soldier's pay being spent on clothes. Writing in the late 1st century AD, Tacitus paints a somewhat gloomy picture of army life: 'military service was burdensome and unprofitable, mind and body were assessed at 10 asses per day: from this they had to buy clothing, weapons and tents, and also to pay off the cruel centurion and buy time off from [fatigue] duty' (*Annals*, I.17).

The best source of evidence for the purchase and supply of clothing comes from Egypt. It appears that orders for clothing issued by the Prefect of Egypt were divided equally amongst the districts to lessen the impact on individual communities. However, we also find that soldiers themselves were able to requisition supplies, and that villages in Egypt were also receiving orders for cloaks and tunics from outside the province. By the reign of Diocletian the manufacture of uniforms was largely concentrated in state factories under the direct supervision of an officer called the *Comes Sacrarum Largitionum.* Even so, documents (e.g. P.Oxy. XII 1448 and P.Cair. Isid. 54) show that clothing was still purchased by the army after that date from small villages in Egypt.

In addition to the regular supplies of issued uniforms, soldiers received clothing from their families. In a private letter found at Karanis in Egypt one Claudius Terentianus, who served in the Alexandrian fleet during the early 2nd century before transferring to a legion, begged his father to send him a new belted tunic. This is because he had worn out his own tunic, probably during training and therefore even before he had properly been enlisted into the army.

While it is accepted that soldiers generally wore tunics made from wool, it is also becoming clear that they certainly owned more than one, with at least one possibly being made from a lighter weight wool or even linen. The historian Plutarch (*Sulla*, XXV) describes the effect that billeting Roman troops had on the local population during the occupation of Asia Minor – roughy, modern Turkey – under that commander: 'Sulla now imposed on Asia as a whole an indemnity of 20,000 talents. At the same time private families were entirely ruined by the brutal behaviour and extortion of the troops quartered on them. Orders were issued that every host should give his guest four tetradrachms a day and should provide for

OPPOSITE **Late Republican and early Imperial tunics in details of fighting figures from the Arch of Orange, dating to the reign of Augustus (31 BC–AD 14). The soldiers' equipment is easily identifiable from other sources, so it is interesting that none of them appear to wear any armour. Just visible on (B) is a knot behind the neck, gathering the neck opening together.**

him an evening meal to which he might invite as many of his friends as he liked. An officer should receive fifty drachmas a day and two suits of clothes, one to wear at home and one to wear when he went out'.

According to Maurikios (*Strat.*, 1.2), soldiers in the eastern Roman army of the 7th century wore tunics made from either rough wool, linen or even goats' hair. Linen especially would be a preferable alternative in hotter climates and also for more formal occasions. There are at least two references to special 'dinner' tunics (*vestis* or *tunica cenatoria*), one in a letter from Vindolanda (Tab. Vindol. II 196), the other a dinner costume given by the Emperor Alexander Severus (AD 222–235) to Maximinus the Younger, recorded in the *Scriptores Historiae Augustae* (SHA, XIX, 30).

Extant papyrus documents from Egypt reveal that bleached or natural-colour linen was favoured for summer garments while wool cloth was worn in winter. An inventory of clothes belonging to Zenon, a manager for Apollonius, finance minister to King Ptolemy II in c.257 BC, gives a good indication of the wardrobes which officials and soldiers might own. Zenon possessed 13 tunics (two of them with sleeves), nine cloaks and four pairs of socks.

Appearance: the sculptural evidence

The complicated tunic folds depicted on some 1st century Rhineland tombstones would seem to suggest that they too were made from a fine material like linen, although this is not supported by archaeological finds. Experiments with both wool and linen reconstructions have failed to replicate this appearance convincingly; simply pulling up the sides does not achieve the desired effect. This leads to a number of conclusions. Firstly, the sculptures themselves may simply illustrate an artistic convention – although other details such as the sidearms appear to be corroborated by archaeological finds. Secondly, the material may have been pleated and ironed, perhaps copying a tradition practised in Ancient Egypt and which may also be discerned in Palmyrene art. Pleating and ironing tunics would obviously be out of the question in the field but is perhaps not too far-fetched for a parade tunic.

Alternatively, the tunic may not be made from one piece but two. Illustrations of the simple kilt worn by gladiators also reveal a curved draped effect, although not as extreme as those seen on the Rhineland tombstones. As gladiators generally wear no upper garment it is possible to see how the draped effect is created: by pulling up surplus material into bunches which are then held in place by a wide waist belt. If soldiers also wore this arrangement it would mean that they would have to wear a short tunic more like a modern T-shirt, under or over a separate kilt. On many of the Rhineland tombstones the drapery on the upper body does not correspond to that on the lower part of the tunic, which could imply that they were separate items. A final possibility is that before the military belts were put on, a waistband – *fascia*

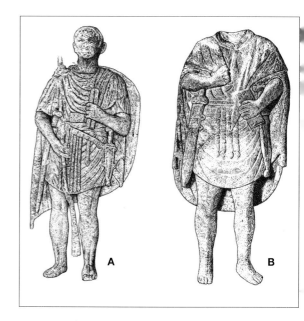

Early Imperial tunics on tombstones from Mainz, Germany.
(A) Publius Flavoleius Cordus, Legio XIIII; his dress, including the *sagum* cloak, is almost identical to that worn by auxiliaries like Daverzus (see page 3), and he too seems to wear a waistband with a document or purse tucked into it.
(B) Unidentified – and it is impossible to state with certainty, just from the soldier's dress, whether he is a legionary or an auxiliary.

ventralis – was worn to flatten the bunching around the waist, thus concealing how the drapes had been produced. These interpretations are purely speculative, however, and any interpretations from sculptural evidence alone are always fraught with difficulties. Unless further evidence is forthcoming the deliberation over the correct design of these tunics may never be resolved.

It is not known to what extent the Rhineland type of tunic was worn elsewhere within the empire but, to judge from the available evidence, this style was only popular from around the beginning to the latter half of the 1st century, when it disappears entirely to be displaced by a simpler, perhaps more utilitarian version. This practical form of tunic clearly existed before the Rhineland examples, as it can be seen on the Arch of Orange (Augustus, 31 BC–AD 14), and on early Principate tombstones from Caesarea in Algeria. It is also the tunic made familiar by its depiction on Trajan's Column (Trajan r.AD 98–117), and the Chatsworth relief (Hadrian, r.AD 117–138), and is clearly the style worn by the Camomile Street soldier from London. The differences between this tunic and those shown on the early Rhineland tombstones are readily apparent: it has a straight lower hem and very few folds at all.

Decoration – *clavi*

An instantly recognisable feature of many surviving tunics from the Roman period are the two contrasting bands of colour known as *clavi* which run from the shoulders to the bottom edges. Although senatorial and equestrian officers would be entitled to purple *clavi* on their tunics, it is not known for certain if ordinary soldiers during the early Principate were allowed to display them. The use of purple clavi by soldiers from the 3rd century onwards, however, is attested both in the *Historia Augustae* (*SHA, Claudius*, XVII, 6) and on wall paintings from Dura Europos.

RIGHT **Early Imperial tunic on the relief of an auxiliary from Caesarea – modern Cherchell, Algeria – dating from the early 1st century AD. The tunic does not display the characteristics of the 'draped' Rhineland examples, and is much plainer.**

FAR RIGHT **Trajan's Column in Rome, celebrating that emperor's Dacian wars at the end of the 1st century AD, has been highly influential in terms of modern perceptions of Roman military dress. This is particularly so in the case of Eastern archers, who are almost invariably depicted today as they are apparently shown on the Column, with long flowing robes.**

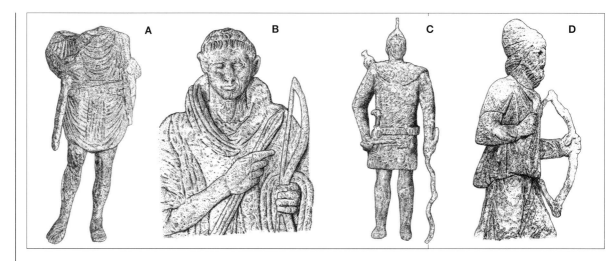

Fuentes believed that some musicians in a gladiatorial scene depicted on a mosaic from Zliten in North Africa may represent members of a military band; these men wear military style yellow-brown cloaks and have short white tunics with black *clavi*. (However, the presence of a female member of the band playing a water-powered organ may cast some doubt on the presumed military status of the others.) A couple of the portrait paintings from Egypt – discussed below – may also show common soldiers, who have tunics which are decorated with either red or black *clavi*.

The *clavi* were woven into the fabrics during manufacture. At Mons Claudianus, Egypt, the majority of *clavi* on textile fragments were between 1cm and 4cm in width, but there were also a number of fragments that had two and three stripes. The *clavi* themselves are sometimes decorated and some of these examples can be around 7cm wide.

The dropped shoulder and 'bunched' neck

On Trajan's Column some scenes seem to illustrate that legionaries involved in construction duties wore a special tunic which was let down from the right shoulder. A similar appearance is found in civilian sources, e.g. representations of blacksmiths. However, modern re-enactors experience little difficulty in working in the basic tunic; and it should also be remembered that soldiers were expected to work in full armour if necessary, so should have been accustomed to any minor inconvenience caused by the tunic. (Might there have been a Roman equivalent of the 'Pioneer Corps' who adopted this fashion? The literary sources seem to contradict the idea.) It seems that under normal circumstances the wide neck opening of the tunic was gathered and fastened together in a small bunch of surplus material at the rear of the neck. This feature is noticeable in a number of scenes on Trajan's Column, and on the mid- to late 2nd century Belvedere Sarcophagus in the Vatican, Rome, where the detail survives clearly enough to strongly suggest that the bunch was tied with a thong rather than pinned together by *fibulae* (brooches). An almost identical arrangement can still be observed today worn by nomadic tribesmen in Mauretania.

There are two apparent disadvantages to wearing a tunic tied into a bunch at the back: it might seem to require assistance in holding and

All these tombstone images of archers show them wearing the same type of clothing as worn by other soldiers: (A) Pantera, of Cohors I Sagittariorum, from Bingerbrück, Germany; (B) Monimus, of Cohors I Ituraeorum, from Tahlbach near Mainz, Germany; (C) from Housesteads, England. (D) is an irregular archer from the Column of Marcus Aurelius, mid-late 2nd century, Rome.

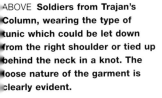

tying, and it is an unnecessary encumbrance when worn beneath armour. The first objection disappears as soon as one watches a woman casually tying her hair up behind without benefit of a mirror. The second seems more serious: nevertheless, the existence of this peculiar fashion is confirmed by its appearance in more than one source, and when reconstructed the bunching at the rear produces all the types of folds observed in the sculptural renditions of military tunics.

Although there are many textile fragments from military sites no complete examples of positively identified military tunics exist. If they were similar in manufacture and design to surviving tunics from this period, e.g. those from Nahal Hever, then another problem presents itself. As the surviving tunics are broader than they are long, this leaves a lot of surplus material beneath the arms. Indeed, this phenomenon can be observed on the Chatsworth relief where the soldiers are shown in their undress uniform of tunic and belts (see page 46). This surplus of material would appear to be an inconvenience, especially when the soldier wore any form of body armour. Modern re-enactors have favoured a narrow tunic, which may therefore be incorrect but which does at least fit comfortably under the armour. This might seem to lend support to the idea that Roman soldiers not only wore a special tunic when they went into action, but that it was of a different design. However, in contradiction of this, recent experiments carried out by members of the Ermine Street Guard indicate that the wide tunic can be worn comfortably beneath armour – indeed, it provides additional padding.

Another feature which can be detected on the Chatsworth relief is what appears to be a narrow strap decorated with studs which passes under the right arm and crosses over the left shoulder. Fuentes confusingly termed this a 'pouch belt' by analogy with those used by 18th/19th century cavalrymen, but suggested that its function was to restrict any blousing of the material which might interfere with the drawing of the sword. Even when wearing an undress uniform soldiers

11

Relief of an olive harvester from Cordoba, Spain. He wears the short-sleeved tunic of the type which could be let down off the shoulder, identical to those worn by some soldiers on Trajan's Column, with the wide neck opening restricted by a large knot tied at the back.

were still equipped with sidearms, generally a sword and dagger. An example of this was vividly brought to light by the discovery of what may well have been a soldier (or perhaps a marine) during the excavations at 1st century Herculaneum. When the man was killed by the eruption of Vesuvius he had been carrying a bag of carpentry tools as well as his trusty sword and two belts, though apparently without a dagger. Shoulder belts decorated with alternate bronze and silver discs can also be seen on the encaustic portraits from Egypt identified as soldiers; but while these are normally identified as sword baldrics, the high angle on the Chatsworth relief would be better explained by Fuentes' suggestion.

Legionaries and auxiliaries

Whereas tombstones of the early Principate show both legionaries and auxiliaries apparently wearing identical tunics, sculptural evidence seems to suggest that this may have changed towards the end of the 1st century. Trajan's Column, in particular, shows the armoured auxiliaries wearing a tunic that is clearly much shorter than those worn by the Roman citizen soldiers. Nevertheless, unarmoured auxiliaries such as the slingers are wearing the same type of tunic as the legionaries. The shorter tunic may therefore be a convenient device to highlight the ethnic character of these soldiers for the benefit of the Roman viewers. A similar emphasis is placed on the auxiliary archers, many of whom wear flowing robes which are generally assumed by modern commentators to represent Middle Eastern costume. Nonetheless, tombstones of archers found in the frontier regions tend to suggest that bowmen, including those from Middle Eastern units, were dressed in much the same manner as other soldiers.

It has been suggested by Bishop that the distinctly un-Roman short tunics worn by some auxiliaries on the Column may have been a result of a change in attitude towards the auxilia after the revolt of the Batavians in AD 69. However, mounted auxiliaries appear to have worn a short tunic from at least the early Principate, well before that revolt – a practice which can also be detected in sculptures of cavalrymen during the Republic. This was possibly because a short tunic would be more practical for riding, especially when worn in combination with trousers, and this practice probably originated with the Celts.

MILITARY CLOAKS

To judge from Imperial sculpture the common soldiers appear to have favoured two distinct types of cloaks – the *paenula* and the *sagum* – while officers of the rank of centurion and above had the option of wearing a more formal style known as a *paludamentum*. In Republican times, according to Livy (VII, 34.9), there was clearly a visible difference between the cloaks worn by officers and their men. He describes how the Tribune Publius Decius and some of his centurions wrapped themselves in common soldiers' cloaks to disguise their rank when they went out on reconnaissance.

The *paenula* was already established in Etruscan times but its origins may have been even earlier. As no surviving examples exist from a positively military context it is only possible to reconstruct its design by

interpreting the available sculptural evidence, but it is best described as a hooded cape. The finest sculptural example from a military context is the tombstone of an unknown soldier found in Camomile Street, London (see page 44). It would seem that the basic design was semi-circular, although an oval shape has also been suggested. The military version of the *paenula* appears to have had a fastened opening at the front, unlike some of its civilian variants such as the *casula* and *cucullus*, which were pulled on over the head. Some *paenula* cloaks appear to have been shorter than others.

In many cases it is unclear from sculptures whether or not they had hoods, although according to Pliny the *paenula* was normally fitted with a long-pointed hood which when not in use hung down on the wearer's back, shaped 'like a bindweed leaf'; and cloaks with this type of hood can be seen on Trajan's Column. Pliny adds (*Nat. Hist.*, XXIV, 18.) that due to the wide neck opening of the *paenula* it was necessary to wear a scarf; and the Camomile Street soldier and a figure from the Adamklissi Tropaeum have evidently followed Pliny's advice.

The four frontal fastenings on the Camomile Street sculpture are extremely clear but somewhat confusing, since two different types are depicted. The top two circular fasteners look like those classed as 'button-and-loop' and were probably bronze, which may in turn have been silvered. Although the third fastener is damaged the bottom one is clearly of a different type, resembling the wooden toggle on a modern duffel coat. The overall accuracy of the sculpture and its attention to detail would seem to rule out the idea that this may be a brooch of some sort. A *paenula* on the Chatsworth relief is entirely fastened with four of these 'toggles' which, if they were brooches, would surely be awkwardly time-consuming to unfasten and refasten. It may not have been too unusual that the

Praetorian Guardsmen shown in sculptures from Italy; all wear *paenula* cloaks. (A) & (B) Arch of Domitian, Puteoli; (C) tombstone, Belgioioso; (D) Cancelleria relief, Rome.

Auxiliaries from Trajan's Column. Points of interest are the fringed cloak, left, and the shortness of both tunics, worn just below the waist. Both men also wear breeches, probably of wool.

Camomile Street soldier had two different types of fastener on his cloak, though the sculptor certainly felt it was worthy of recording for posterity.

Both the *sagum* and its shorter derivative, the *sagulum*, were simply rectangular pieces of heavy woollen material. The papyrus document BGU 1564 includes an order for four cloaks each 6 cubits (2.66m) long and 4 cubits (1.77m) wide. These measurements can be compared with a surviving cloak from Nubia which was 1.75m long x 1.05m wide; one from Nahal Hever (no.43) which was 2.70m long x 1.40m wide; and another example from Thorsberg in Schleswig-Holstein, Germany, which measured 2.50m long x 1.68m wide. The document records that the cloaks should weigh 3¾ minae (1.6kg), and each cost 24 drachmae (6 denarii).

The cloaks in BGU 1564 were identical in size to a blanket recorded in the same document that was destined for the hospital, although the blanket was heavier and cost 28 drachmae (7 denarii). Cloaks of this size were therefore quite broad and could easily be wrapped around the body for extra warmth. A further suggestion of large size is provided by the legend associated with St Martin (c.AD 371–397) when he was serving as a tribune at Amiens. One bitterly cold day Martin saw a beggar outside the city gates and, moved by his plight, cut his own cloak in two and offered half to the beggar.

In the 1st century AD the poet Martial (*Epig*, VIII, 58) lampooned a man called Artemidorus, saying that as he wore thick cloaks he should have been named '*sagaris*'. In contrast there were also lighter versions of the *sagum* which could be worn in summer or indoors. The cloaks seen on the Rhineland tombstones have almost as many folds as the tunics, which might suggest that they were of a relatively light material.

The *sagum* was fastened at the right shoulder by means of a brooch, and this is one reason for the large numbers of brooches found on military sites. The Roman historian Varro (*D.L.*, V, 167) claimed that the *sagum* was of Gallic origin and had been adopted by the Romans during the Celtic wars of the 4th century BC; but it is also present in German and Spanish contexts. The *sagum* was therefore another example of the Romans borrowing what was originally a barbarian form of dress and making it their own.

It seems that the *sagum* was especially popular with the military and was worn by all ranks from common soldier to emperor. It is by far the most common type of cloak represented on Trajan's Column. In fact the *sagum* became so associated with the army that the phrase 'putting on the military *sagum*' was analogous with 'going to war'. It was because of this militaristic association that the pacific Emperor Marcus Aurelius later tried unsuccessfully to ban its use (*SHA*, VI, 27). A recently translated document discovered in Carlisle refers to ten military cloaks, *saga militaria*. This is far from a unique reference, as 'military cloaks' are also specifically mentioned by Appian

Paenula cloak from Egypt, of uncertain date. It is in a 1.2 twill weave; a curved hem has been turned back and finished with braid. (University of Pennsylvania Museum, E16803)

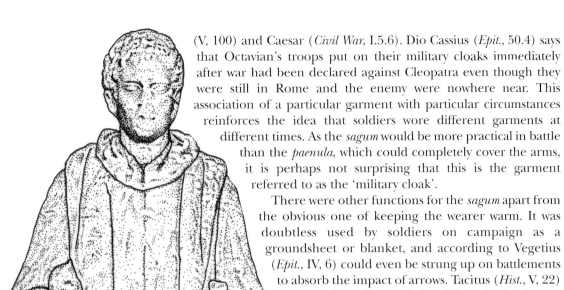

(V, 100) and Caesar (*Civil War*, I.5.6). Dio Cassius (*Epit.*, 50.4) says that Octavian's troops put on their military cloaks immediately after war had been declared against Cleopatra even though they were still in Rome and the enemy were nowhere near. This association of a particular garment with particular circumstances reinforces the idea that soldiers wore different garments at different times. As the *sagum* would be more practical in battle than the *paenula*, which could completely cover the arms, it is perhaps not surprising that this is the garment referred to as the 'military cloak'.

There were other functions for the *sagum* apart from the obvious one of keeping the wearer warm. It was doubtless used by soldiers on campaign as a groundsheet or blanket, and according to Vegetius (*Epit.*, IV, 6) could even be strung up on battlements to absorb the impact of arrows. Tacitus (*Hist.*, V, 22) relates that when rebel soldiers broke into a Roman camp during the revolt of the Batavians, the Romans were so taken by surprise that they had to wrap cloaks around their forearms to act as shields. Tacitus also writes (*Hist.*, V, 23) that on another occasion the Batavians themselves had even resorted to using their cloaks as sails.

It is a matter of debate as to whether cloaks could be worn in battle. Julius Caesar certainly did, which was one way that he was instantly recognisable; and this may imply that the rest of his men did not. During his flight from the battle for the Pharos at Alexandria, Caesar lost his cloak, which was subsequently carried off by the Alexandrians as a highly prized trophy (*Appian*, II, 90). On Trajan's Column soldiers engaged in battle fight without cloaks. However, the Roman soldiers killed when a countermine collapsed during the siege of Dura Europos in c.AD 256 were wearing cloaks at the time, as their cloak brooches survived.

A number of cloaks depicted on Trajan's Column and elsewhere clearly have at least one fringed edge. It is not certain if this was a sign of status but it does appear to be associated with higher grade troops including Praetorians, *beneficiarii*, cavalrymen, standard bearers, and senior officers such as tribunes. Other sculptures indicate that some cloaks were decorated with tassels at the bottom corners (see page 47 and Plate G1).

Senior officers were entitled to wear the special cloak called a *paludamentum*. This was worn draped over the left shoulder and partially over the left arm. As such it was evidently more a mark of rank rather than a practical campaign garment, and officers are equally likely to be seen wearing the more functional *sagum*. The *paludamentum* appears to have been rectangular like the *sagum*, although it has been suggested from sculptural evidence that the lower corners may have been cut away and rounded off.

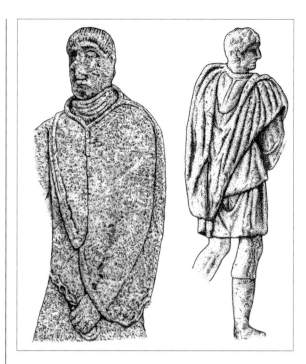

LEFT **Soldier in a *paenula* cloak – apparently hooded – and scarf, in a detail from the Adamklissi monument.**

RIGHT **Detail from Scene LXXXVI on Trajan's Column, showing unarmoured soldiers on the march. This man wears a *paenula* cloak with the hood visibly thrown back and both sides thrown up onto his shoulders.**

***Paenula* cloak pattern, 1.95m long x 3.1m wide. (After H.Granger-Taylor)**

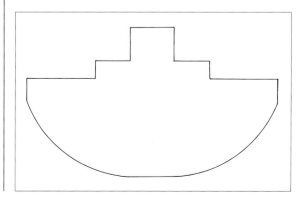

DYES AND DYEING

The Romans inherited a range of dyeing techniques and traditions from across the Empire. Initially this would have been in the form of goods supplied as part of a levy. Livy records that the newly conquered territories of Spain, Sardinia and Sicily had to supply clothing to the army of Scipio in Africa (XXIX, 36, & XXX, 3). But as new provinces became more organised specialist craftsmen, including dye workers, would be exploited by the Romans; for instance, Pliny states that Gaul was famous for its extensive range of dyestuffs (*Nat. Hist.*, XXII.2).

The majority of dyes were vegetable in origin and some required a mordant to fix the dye to the fibre. Mordants were usually common minerals, in particular alum, or iron salts, which could be obtained by using rusty nails. The useful side effects of this process were that alum enhanced the brightness of the dye while iron extended the colour range. Other colours could be achieved by vat dyeing, fermenting and oxydising the fibres with the dye. The best-known colour achieved with this technique was the blue obtained from woad (*isatis tinctoria*), which is actually a similar colour constituent to the much rarer indigo.

Madder (*rubia tinctorum*) was the most common red dyestuff in the Roman world. In places like Britain where madder was unknown at that time the Romans would have imported it in dried form. However, bedstraw, a herbaceous plant, in particular 'lady's bedstraw' (*galium verum*) was probably a local alternative. After mordanting, madder could also produce other colours ranging from a peach-yellow to a brown-purple.

True purple could only be produced by specialist dyeworkers in the eastern Mediterranean, particularly in the area around Tyre, home of the shellfish *murex brandaris* and *murex trunculus* – two types of whelk which secreted the precious dye fluid. Their rarity, together with the dye's fastness to light and washing, was the reason why purple was so prized as an exclusive status symbol. According to Pliny (*Nat. Hist.*, 137) one Cornelius Nepos, who died during the reign of Augustus, was supposed to have said that in his youth violet-coloured shellfish dye was fashionable in Rome and cost about 100 denarii a pound; however, this was later followed by the double-dyed Tyrian variety which could not be bought for less than 1,000 denarii a pound. Such garments were clearly well beyond the reach of the average legionary, who in the late 1st century AD earned about 300 denarii a year. However, senior officers came from senatorial families, whose wealth during the early Empire might be extraordinary (and even the topmost levels of the centurionate sometimes achieved very considerable riches).

Nevertheless, the demand for purple predictably led to the creation of a number of cheaper alternatives, and a counterfeit industry like that which exploits today's hunger for 'designer labels'. The poet Ovid remarked that it was madness to wear expensive purples when there were so many cheaper alternatives (*Ars. Am.*, III, 170). Cicero mockingly observed that wool taken from sheep reared in Canusium, which was brown with a reddish hue, served as the poor man's purple.

A purple of sorts could easily be achieved by simply over-dyeing red from madder with blue from indigo or woad. Archil, a purple dye obtained by fermenting lichen in stale urine, was also widely used. Evidence of 'faked' purple clothing was brought to light by discoveries in the Bar Kochba caves in Israel.

Elsewhere in these caves were examples of tunics dyed yellow with saffron. The Romans may have deemed yellow inappropriate as a martial colour because of its associations with the veil traditionally worn by brides on their wedding day. This prejudice is highlighted by Virgil (*Aeneid*, XI, 777) when Chloreus, a former priest of Cybele and therefore a eunuch, assumes the role of a soldier. Because he wears a cloak of yellow and other bright garments he is described somewhat disparagingly as a fop rather than a true warrior.

Wool was easier to dye than linen, which was invariably left its natural shade or bleached in sunlight. However, wool could also be left in its variety of natural colours from the sheep in different regions. Checked effects such as those popular with the Celts could therefore be produced by mixing the wool from different sheep (naturally, some Roman writers viewed garments produced in this manner as unsuitable for civilised people).

A typical cavalryman depicted on Trajan's Column. He wears a fringed *sagum* cloak over his dagged mail shirt, short tunic and calf-length breeches.

CATALOGUE OF THE EVIDENCE FOR THE COLOUR OF MILITARY TUNICS AND CLOAKS

The development of 'practical history' groups since 1972 has increased general interest in the colours of Roman clothing and textiles. Unfortunately, due to the scarcity of accessible published material, and a former trend amongst historians to relegate or even ignore the study of textile finds, there has been a tendency to follow preconceptions rather than specific archaeological data.

Undoubtedly the most controversial aspect of Roman military tunics is their colour. The traditional view is that legionaries wore red, and this was the colour adopted by the early Roman re-enactors. Contrary to this idea, Fuentes suggested that legionaries and senior officers wore white, while centurions were dressed in red to make them instantly recognisable. To judge from recent publications, both popular and academic, this view seems to have been widely accepted. However, many re-enactors do not concur with this viewpoint, and as a result the public is now presented with a confusing array of soldiers in tunics coloured either red, white, blue, green or yellow.

While there is no doubt that the Romans had the capability of producing all these colours, the issue is whether any or all were adopted by the army. It should be remembered that it is impossible to specifically identify textile fragments as belonging to military tunics, including those from supposedly military sites. There is a tendency to forget that there were many civilians present in and around forts; and, perhaps more basically, that the Romans had as many uses for textiles other than for clothes as we do today.

An attempt has been made here to address this imbalance and to present without bias all the evidence that is currently available. By and large, readers are ultimately left to draw their own conclusions as to how this evidence is best interpreted; but a summary is included in the forthcoming second part of this study, Men-at-Arms 390.

(1) Historical fresco, tomb on the Esquiline, Rome; Republican period

This fragment of a tomb fresco is probably among the oldest surviving examples of Roman painting, and provides us with the earliest clues for the colour of Roman military tunics. It appears to illustrate an event in c.326 BC during the Samnite wars. Around the main central group of figures can be seen a number of warriors in short white tunics and kilts. Becatti dates this fresco to the 1st century BC, but adds that it appears to be a copy of a much earlier work. It may depict the historical event described but this is not certain.

According to Livy (IX, 40, 2–3 & IX, 40, 9), one division of the Samnite army wore bleached white linen tunics, adopted because they had consecrated themselves and white was the colour of the priesthood. Unfortunately Livy neglected to leave us a description of contemporary Roman army tunics. An Etruscan fresco dating to the 4th century BC may provide a clue. The so-called 'Francois' tomb shows a legendary battle possibly between the Etruscans and the Romans, or at least their Latin allies. A soldier in a bronze muscle cuirass and a red tunic is being killed by a naked opponent. As the defeated warrior is unlikely to be an Etruscan this could reasonably be seen as evidence for the colour of Roman tunics at this period.

(2) Historical fresco, tomb of the Statilii, Rome; Republican period

This may also show Roman soldiers from the early Republic. The details of the costumes, such as the short white kilts, are similar to the earlier Esquiline fresco, so this too may be a copy of a much earlier work. It is therefore possible that this painting also represents another legendary battle between Romans and Samnites, but there is no general agreement as to which historical event is depicted.

(3) Silius Italicus, IX, 420; late Republic

The poet Silius Italicus records that the cloaks for lictors were red while those used by senior commanders were either purple or white.

(4) *African War*, LVII, 54–6; late Republic

Q.Caecilius Scipio, commander of the Pompeian forces in Africa, always

The Emperor Marcus Aurelius (r.AD 161–180) as commander-in-chief, from a statue now in the Baltimore Art Gallery. He has a *paludamentum* fastened on his left shoulder, draped around his back, carried forward across the midriff and draped over the left arm.

wore a purple cloak. This apparently angered his African ally, the Numidian king Juba I, because this was his own normal attire; subsequently Scipio was obliged to dress in white.

(5) Plutarch (c.AD50–120), *Lives*, Crassus, 23

On the eve of the fateful battle of Carrhae (53 BC), Crassus mistakenly wore a black cloak. Not surprisingly this was interpreted as a bad omen, and Crassus had to revert to wearing a purple cloak. Why he should choose to wear black instead of the general's colour is unexplained.

(6) Mosaic, Palestrina, Italy; date uncertain

The next two subjects, the Palestrina mosaic and the 'Judgement of Solomon' fresco, are perhaps the most controversial as together they formed the cornerstone of Fuentes' hypothesis on Roman tunic colours, in particular for those of the Praetorian Guard and centurions.

The Palestrina mosaic (see this page) shows an Egyptian landscape with the Nile in flood and numerous exotic African animals. At the lower centre a group of soldiers are gathered around what is clearly a temple. Fuentes referred to the date of this mosaic as ranging from anywhere between the 1st century BC and the 3rd century AD, but believed that the mosaic documented a visit to Egypt by Octavian (later the Emperor Augustus) after the battle of Actium in 31 BC. Octavian's visit coincided with an abundant flooding of the Nile which the mosaic seems to record. Nevertheless, other scholars are of the opinion that the mosaic is in fact a copy of a much earlier work by an Alexandrian school, that no longer survives (this theory was most recently stated by Meyboom in his detailed study of the mosaic).

It should be noted that there are slight discrepancies in the details of uniform colours between the observations of Fuentes and Meyboom, in particular regarding the figures Fuentes believed to be the admiral Agrippa and his centurion bodyguard. For example, Fuentes described one man (Agrippa) as wearing a very pale blue tunic and moulded cuirass, and accompanied by another figure dressed in a red, sleeveless, knotted tunic (a centurion). Meyboom, however, describing the same two figures, refers to a soldier who wears a white leather or linen muscle cuirass over a white *chiton* (a Greek-style tunic), while the other is dressed in a brownish-yellow *chiton*.

There is some evidence that the colour blue was, perhaps not surprisingly, associated both with the sea and the navy. Thus Fuentes believed that the figure wearing what he thought was a blue tunic could well have been the admiral

From the Palestrina Mosaic, Italy (item 6 in the text catalogue) – a close-up of the group of figures frequently identified as Praetorian Guardsmen, standing before an Egyptian temple. A reddish tunic tied at the back of the neck is visible on the central figure. (Copyright Fratelli Alinari)

Item 7 in the text catalogue: pygmies dressed as military figures, from the late Republican 'Judgement of Solomon' fresco, Pompeii. The armour and equipment reflect designs commonly used throughout the Eastern Mediterranean world in the Hellenistic era. The right-hand figure is dressed entirely in red clothing, with a red helmet crest.

Agrippa. According to Suetonius (*Augustus*, 25) Agrippa was in fact honoured by Octavian, who presented him with a blue flag.

The historian Appian (V, 100) records that in somewhat similar circumstances Sextus Pompey took to wearing a blue cloak because of his victories at sea. What appears to be the only other reference in Roman literature to blue military tunics is when the historian Vegetius (*Epit.*, IV, 37), writing in the 4th century AD, tells us that the sailors in the British fleet dyed not only their tunics but also the sails of their ships to match the colour of the sea.

One of the figures in the Palestrina mosaic that has been obviously restored is the character Fuentes identified as Octavian. He appears to wear a green moulded linen or leather cuirass – possibly with attached groin flaps, *pteruges* – over a white *chiton*. While moulded linen or leather cuirasses are not always thought of as being Roman, these details do correspond to other Macedonian tomb paintings from Egypt. Taking this into consideration with the other evidence, including details of the soldiers' dress (e.g. Greek-style boots, *embades*, rather than Roman *caligae*, plus the Egyptian setting), Meyboom concluded that the figures on the mosaic in fact represent members of the elite troops of the Ptolemaic army, the Macedones.

(7) 'The Judgement of Solomon', fresco, Pompeii, Italy; late Republican/early Imperial

Fuentes argued that this court scene enacted by pygmies (see this page) echoed contemporary dress. However, once more it is believed that this fresco is a copy of an earlier Alexandrian work and that therefore the contemporary dress is Ptolemaic rather than Roman. Fuentes asserted that two of the soldiers wear white tunics, although at first glance the tunic of the soldier about to cleave the baby in half appears to be light blue; Sekunda in fact states that this tunic is blue. However, the fresco is badly damaged in places, including areas around this figure in particular. What appears as blue may in fact be an attempt to render shading on a white garment, a technique that is evident elsewhere on the fresco.

The second soldier has a salmon-pink cloak. A third soldier wears a dark red tunic and cloak, which Fuentes believed marked him out as an officer, most likely a centurion. Nevertheless, all three soldiers have similar red helmet crests, which would seem to weaken this theory. Vegetius, writing in the 4th century AD, records that centurions wore transverse silvered crests to distinguish them in battle, but he does not mention them wearing a different tunic colour as well. The crest of the third soldier is certainly not transverse, nor does he show any of the usual attributes associated with centurions such as the vine stick or greaves. However, this soldier's armour and helmet are different in colour from those of his companions, so Fuentes may be correct in identifying this man as an officer. But of which army?

(8) Tavern sign, Pompeii, Italy; late Republican/early Imperial

This wall painting (see this page) shows a soldier being offered wine by the landlord. Apparently off duty, he wears only a tunic and cloak but appears to carry a spear which could well be a weighted *pilum*. If so, this soldier would certainly be a legionary or a Praetorian rather than a local policeman; he is in fact similar in overall appearance to the contemporary soldiers, probably Praetorians, on the Cancelleria relief in Rome.

The soldier's cloak is clearly of the *paenula* style and is a yellow-brown colour, apparently worn over a grey-green scarf. An alternative colour for the *paenula* may be suggested both by a tombstone with some painted details surviving, found at Castleford in Yorkshire, and the remains of a cloak found with a bog body also discovered in Yorkshire in the 19th century. In both cases the cloak was green, although it must be stressed that the identification of either subject as a soldier is doubtful. A more positive suggestion is supplied by one of the Vindolanda writing tablets, which refers to a white *paenula*. In view of some of the later evidence from Dura Europos discussed below, this conceivably belonged to the commanding officer of the cohort.

(9) Wall painting, House of Valerius Rufus (or of the Trojan Shrine); Region I, Ins.6.4., Pompeii, Italy; late Republican/early Imperial

In the upper registers of a painting are two figures, a male and a female. The former is armoured and wears a Montefortino-style helmet with a red crest, a white linen cuirass and bronze greaves. He carries a large oval shield and a spear in his left hand, and adjusts his cloak with the other. His tunic is a pinkish-red and the cloak is white. Although the figure is probably meant to represent a deity or a hero he appears to be depicted in a contemporary panoply, which in fact looks very similar to the figure reg-arded as Mars on the Altar of Domitius Aheno-barbus. This is supported by the inclusion of a Monte-fortino helmet rather than a stylised Attic type.

(10) Historical fresco, Pompeii, Italy; late Republican/early Imperial

One more scene from Pompeii, which shows a

Details of frescos from Pompeii (items 8 and 10 in the text catalogue). Left, a soldier in a yellow-brown *paenula* cloak with dark red-brown *clavi* and a grey-green scarf is drinking at a tavern. Although the fresco is damaged it is just possible that traces of a white tunic are visible beneath the hem of the cloak and at the soldier's left sleeve. Hellenistic artists frequently did not paint in white areas, they simply drew an outline on the unpainted plaster and left it blank. The right-hand figure is usually described as a traveller, but his appearance is very military. He wears a yellow-brown *sagum* cloak over a white tunic.

man talking to a woman or sorceress at the roadside, perhaps deserves a mention (see page 21). The man is wearing a short white belted tunic under a yellow-brown cloak and he rests on a spear or staff. The similarity between his apparel and that of off-duty soldiers is obvious, although this figure is generally referred to in modern texts simply as a traveller.

(11) Fresco, Domus Aurea, Rome, Italy; early Imperial

A male armoured figure depicted in a fresco from Nero's Golden House possibly represents the Trojan hero Hector (see page 46). Although the overall impression of the panoply is Hellenistic – his helmet is of a pseudo-Corinthian design, his shield is oval and he carries a spear – the body armour appears to be a '*lorica segmentata*' (which in itself is worthy of further investigation). For the purpose of this study, the warrior wears a green tunic and a red cloak. A suggestion by J.P.Wild that green would normally be considered rather expensive for soldiers' uniforms need not apply to a profligate ruler like Nero, and by extension to the Praetorian Guard. Given the clear association of the Golden House with Nero, it is tempting to speculate that the figure represents a member of that infamous corps, and that during his reign the Imperial bodyguard were dressed not only in Hellenistic style to suit Nero's passion for all things Greek, but also in the colour of the circus faction that he fanatically supported – the Greens.

A wax encaustic portrait from Egypt (item 23 in the text catalogue), which may provide further evidence that the wearing of red cloaks was much more widespread than previously believed. The man wears a sword on his right side – the white, perhaps ivory pommel with a bronze terminal is just visible; and this position is usually an indication of the common soldier of the early Imperial period. The Antonine hairstyle would appear to indicate a date in the latter part of the 2nd century AD, a date which supports the belief that his sword position is not that of a centurion. His tunic is white, with red *clavi*, and over his left shoulder he wears a red *sagum* cloak which partially obscures his sword belt with its alternate bronze and silver studs. (The Manchester Museum, The University of Manchester)

(12) Isidore of Seville (c.AD 650); *Origines*, XIX, xxii, 10

In the 7th century AD, St Isidore wrote a history of the world up to his own times. Referring to a period when Rome was 'under the Consuls' – presumably the Republican era – he wrote that there was a dye, *russata*, which was called 'Phoenicea' by the Greeks and was known as *coccina* in his own day. He claims it was invented by the Spartans to conceal blood when they were wounded in battle, so as not to encourage their enemies. We must therefore conclude that the dye was red in colour. Isidore adds that Roman soldiers also used it, 'whence [they] were called *russati*'. This can be taken to mean that the soldiers themselves were nicknamed *russati*; but can also be translated as 'whence the *russati* took their name', which could allude instead to the Red circus faction.

Isidore further implies that Roman soldiers only wore this colour on the eve and actual day of battle, and that before a battle the same colour was possibly displayed in front of the headquarters tent. This reminds us of the actions of Caesar (*Gallic War*, II, 4, & *Civil Wars*, III, 89, and Plutarch, *Pompey*, 68), who hoisted a battle flag both when the Nervii attacked his camp and before the battle of Pharsalus – although it is most interesting to note that in Plutarch's account he says that it was a tunic that was displayed.

Taken at face value, Isidore suggests that Roman soldiers wore red only into battle, and presumably therefore wore another colour for normal wear. Although it is believed that Isidore used ancient Roman sources now lost, and authors such as Tacitus and Suetonius, he is not always considered to be very reliable. Therefore we have no idea of the accuracy of his observations or his grasp of military knowledge.

(13) Quintilianus (c.AD 35–95?), *Declamationes*, III Declamatio, 'Pro Milite Contra Tribunum'

The rhetorician Quintilianus, in the passage 'For a soldier against a tribune', set during the period of the army of C.Marius, gives a vivid picture of the dress of a Roman soldier of the late Republic or even perhaps the 1st century AD. Quintilianus describes how the soldier's body was protected by a sword, hard iron armour and a helmet which covered the face; he added that the helmet crest was designed to 'strike terror' into the enemy, and that the name of Marius was inscribed upon their shields. Finally he states that the men also wore 'the terrible dress of the god of war', Mars.

The tunic worn by Mars is shown in Roman art as a red colour, e.g. in the mosaic preserved in the Villa Borghese, Italy, where priests offer a sacrifice before the god. The red tunics of the circus faction were also dedicated to Mars; so the clear implication from this passage is that soldiers wore red tunics into battle.

(14) Tacitus (c.AD 56–?), *Histories*, II, 89

Writing about the triumphal entry into Rome by the Emperor Vitellius in AD 69, Tacitus describes how the legionary camp prefects, tribunes and senior centurions were dressed in shining white, *candida vesta*. Fuentes believed that if the centurions and other senior officers were specially dressed in shining white on this occasion, they must therefore have worn another colour at other times. Basing his interpretation on the evidence from the Palestrina mosaic and the 'Judgement of Solomon' fresco, Fuentes ignored the possibility that the other colour may have been off-white or unbleached cloth, and concluded that the alternative colour was red. However, some doubt has now been cast on these sources, in particular as reliable evidence for Roman army tunic colours.

What is more evident is that soldiers had additional tunics, one of which could possibly be specially whitened for events like the triumphal parade of Vitellius. Another occasion when soldiers might be expected to wear their best uniform would be the Saturnalia festival. A list of household goods and clothing on one of the Vindolanda writing tablets mentions a tunic for dining, conceivably for the Saturnalia dinner or some other special banquet. (It is on this same list that the white *paenula* cloak mentioned above appears.)

(15) Textiles, Vindolanda, Britain; late 1st century AD

Out of a sample of nearly 100 textile fragments from Vindolanda, 50 were analysed for dye, and evidence was found on only nine of these. Many of the other textiles were of unpigmented wool and therefore suitable for dying, but had been too heavily stained from burial to show any trace of dye. Of the nine textiles analysed, eight were dyed red; the other

A

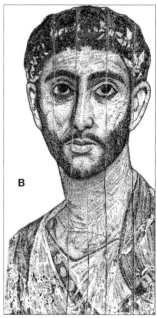

B

Two more wax encaustic portraits from Egypt dating between the reigns of Trajan (AD 98–117) and Antoninus Pius (AD 138–161). Both men are identified as soldiers and wear white tunics with dark blue cloaks on their left shoulders. (A) seems to be a common soldier, since a sword pommel is just visible on his right side. In contrast, (B) has a sword belt crossing his right shoulder, so at this date he could be a centurion. His tunic has black *clavi*; he also wears a gilt wreath – see Plate G2.

appeared to have been a purple stripe. The red dye used was almost certainly madder, *rubia tinctorum*, which in the case of Britain would have had to be imported. While a report on the Vindolanda textiles concluded that the picture of Roman soldiers in red tunics may well be correct, we should remember that the textile fragments are extremely small and may not be exclusively from tunics at all. A recently translated document from Vindolanda actually refers to purple and red curtains...

(16) New Testament Gospels, *Matthew*, 28, 28; 1st century AD

It is perhaps of more than passing interest that the cloak the auxiliary soldiers of the Jerusalem garrison used to mock Christ, as documented by Matthew, was red. The reed stick and the crown of thorns immediately recall the vine stick that centurions carried, and the crowns of leaves that could be awarded to these officers. When the soldiers flogged Christ could they have been vicariously getting their own back on someone else? The other Gospels all refer to a purple cloak. Under the circumstances a red cloak is far more likely to have been readily available, but it is obvious in what connotation the other Gospel writers regarded the significance of a purple cloak.

(17) Martial, *Epigrams*, XIV, 129; 1st century AD

When Martial described red Canusian cloaks he said that Rome wore brown, the Gauls red, but that this was a colour which boys and soldiers also liked, although it is not clear whether Martial meant all soldiers.

(18) Pliny the Elder (AD 23/4–79), *Natural History*, XX, 3; 1st century AD

Pliny records that scarlet dye from the kermes was used for dyeing the *paludamentum*, the distinctive officer's cloak. He mentions that the most commonly used red dye, madder, was grown near Rome; but that the most prestigious red dye was obtained from the kermes (*kermococcus vermilio*), a parasitic insect which infests the kermes oak throughout southern Europe. He wrongly believed that the dye came from the berries of the tree; it was in fact obtained from the female insects' egg sacks.

While red cloaks are invariably thought of as belonging to generals – e.g. Caesar (*Gallic War*, VII, 5) – even here we must exercise caution. When Sextus Pompeius (died c.36 BC) changed the colour of his cloak to blue as mentioned above, Appian (died c.AD 165) says that he changed it from the purple that commanders usually wore (V, 100). Overall, however, there seems to be some confusion in texts both ancient and modern as to the point on the spectrum at which 'red' becomes purple.

(19) Tombstone (CIL xiii 6277), Mainz, Germany; 1st century AD

A rare example of a tombstone that survived with some of its original colouring may possibly indicate that the practice of wearing red cloaks was more widespread among ordinary soldiers. Although the paint did not survive for long it was possible to determine that either Silius, a cavalry trooper in the Ala Picentiana, or his attendant (*calo*), had a red cloak. Meanwhile the remains of paint on another tombstone, that of Gnaeus Musius, the *aquilifer* standard-bearer with Legio XIIII Gemina Martia Victrix, led the German archaeologists who were creating a reconstruction of the monument to restore the tunic as white.

 continued on page 33

THE FALL OF THE REPUBLIC
1: Gaius Julius Caesar, c.57 BC
2: Marcus Licinius Crassus, c.53 BC
3: Sextus Pompeius (died c.36 BC)

A

GUARDIANS OF THE NORTH
1: Legionary, Germany, AD 14
2: Auxiliary, Germany, AD 20–50
3: *Beneficiarius*, Britain, AD 70

B

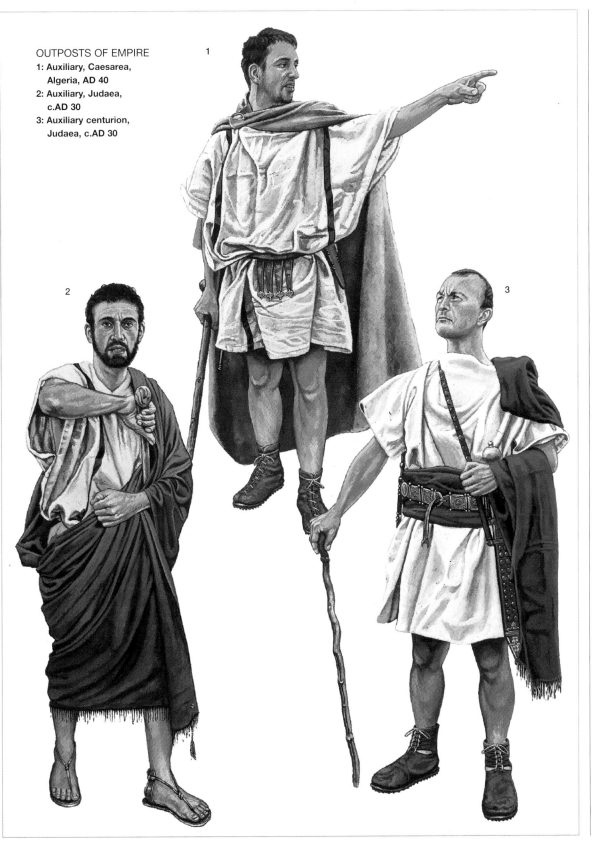

OUTPOSTS OF EMPIRE
1: Auxiliary, Caesarea, Algeria, AD 40
2: Auxiliary, Judaea, c.AD 30
3: Auxiliary centurion, Judaea, c.AD 30

C

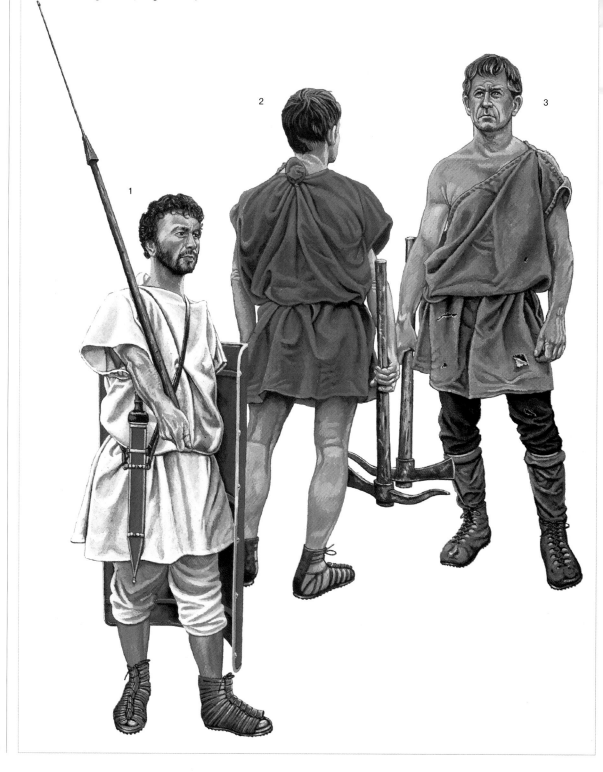

EXPANDING THE EMPIRE
1: Legionary, Dacian wars, late 1st century AD
2 & 3: Legionaries, fatigue dress, Dacian Wars

1

2

3

D

E

THE POWER BEHIND THE THRONE
1, 2 & 3: Praetorian Guards, 1st–2nd centuries AD

F

POLICING THE GREEK EAST
1: Marine, Athens, mid-2nd century AD
2: Centurion, Alexandria, mid-2nd century AD
3: *Diogmitoi*, Ephesos, 2nd century AD

G

SERVANTS OF ROME
1: Legionary under punishment, 1st–2nd centuries AD
2: Senior tribune, 2nd century AD
3: Commander of auxiliary cohort, 1st–2nd centuries AD

FORTVNAE
VEXILLA
TIONES
LEG.II.AVG.
LEG.VI.VIC.
P.S.P.L.L.

H

(20) Pay receipt and textiles, Masada, Israel; 1st century AD

A recently excavated receipt sheds light on military tunics, and seems to confirm that even ordinary soldiers owned more than one. The receipt belonged to C.Messius, son of Gaius of the Fabian tribe, recruited from Beirut. In spite of his local origin it is believed that he served in Legio X Fretensis, possibly as a cavalryman, rather than in an auxiliary unit. Among the list of compulsory deductions from his pay were 7 denarii for a linen tunic, and an unspecified amount for a white tunic. Cotton and Geiger suggested that as linen would have been an expensive item to purchase, this garment would have been kept for special occasions. However, we could expect that in Eastern climates soldiers may have preferred linen to woollen garments. For instance, during the Persian wars of the 4th century, Ammianus Marcellinus (XIX, 8.8) describes how he and a companion tore up their linen clothes to make a line so that they could lower a cap into a well to obtain water.

A number of linen and wool fragments were also uncovered during the excavations at Masada; these must, however, be treated with great caution as possible evidence for Roman army tunics. Many of the textiles would undoubtedly have belonged to the Jewish defenders and civilians present at the siege, and some of the fragments were clearly not from clothing at all. Nearly all of the linen textiles were left undyed but it was not clear how white they would have been originally. It is therefore fairly safe to suggest that the linen tunic mentioned in the Masada pay receipt was white. A true white had probably only been achieved by one textile fragment, which had been made from lamb's wool.

By way of contrast, more than half of the 105 wool textiles that were analysed had been dyed. Of these 14 were red, which ranged in shade from a salmon-pink to dark maroon, while six other examples were either plain blue or blue-green. Contrasting colour bands in dark blue, purple or mauve were observed on several fragments. It was noted that most of the coloured textiles would originally have been worn by women, and this is supported by Jewish literature and the Egyptian funerary portraits from the Roman period, where men's tunics are almost without exception white. However, one textile fragment, consisting of two thick selvedges which had been sewn together and dyed red, was believed to come from a man's tunic, and with reference to Fuentes' article it was thought possibly a military one. But at least one Egyptian funeral portrait depicts a woman in a scarlet-red tunic, so once more this evidence is inconclusive. In addition, while Jewish law forbade men from wearing coloured tunics there is evidence that, like the Romans, Jewish people did not always follow the rules. The Babylonian Talmud refers to a Jewish man who wore a new Roman red tunic while within a period of mourning.

We owe much of our knowledge on the Roman army from this period to the Jewish historian Josephus, who participated in the war, was captured, and later collaborated with the Romans. In describing the fall of Jerusalem he relates how one of the main Jewish leaders, Simon

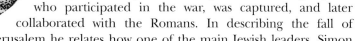

Part of a tombstone from Vienna, Austria, commemorating Titus Flavius Draccus. He was a cavalryman, serving with Ala I Flavia Domitiana Britannica Milliaria Civium Romanorum – a thousand-strong British regiment, honoured for outstanding service during the German or Dacian campaigns of the Emperor Domitian (AD 81–96) with a block grant of Roman citizenship. The tombstone had traces of original blue colouring still surviving on Draccus' upper garment.

Bar Gioras, tried to tunnel out of the city with some of his followers, but was unable to get past the Roman lines. It appears that Simon tried – unsuccessfully – to bluff his way past Roman guards by disguising himself as either a Roman soldier or an officer, for he wore a number of white tunics and a reddish purple cloak (*BJ*, 7.26–36). Interestingly, the combination of a white tunic with a red or purple cloak will appear several times later.

(21) Papyri, Egypt; 2nd century AD

Among the huge collection of ancient documents discovered in Egypt in a remarkable state of preservation are at least two papyri which refer to the delivery of clothing to provincial armies. Together they support the belief that local communities supplied the army; nevertheless, it is interesting to note that villages in Egypt were supplying troops as far away as Judaea and Cappadocia (now part of modern Turkey). There is, however, other evidence that the sending or collecting of military supplies over great distances was not unusual. A strength report of c.AD 105 relating to Cohors I Veterana Hispanorum Equitata, found in Egypt but probably dating to a period when the unit was based in Macedonia, actually records that soldiers had been sent all the way to Gaul (France) to obtain clothing.

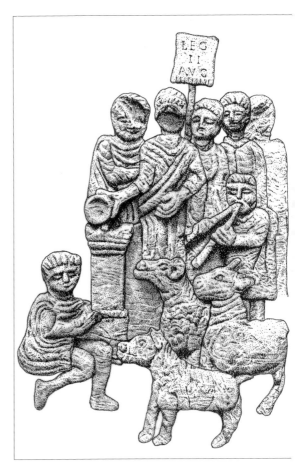

Fuentes found it surprising that one of these Egyptian documents recording the delivery of 19 tunics for the 'guards and soldiers' serving in Judaea also referred to five white cloaks. This seemed to contradict the other pictorial evidence, which largely suggested that military cloaks in general should be yellow-brown. However, the papyrus document BGU 1564 also refers to four white cloaks, providing the additional term 'Syrian'. To these can now be added the white cloak from the Vindolanda document, and two white cloaks on the fresco from Dura Europos (to be discussed in the forthcoming second volume of this study); while another papyrus from a slightly later date in fact mentions the 'controllers of tunics and white cloaks'.

There is another point of interest, bearing in mind that Roman military documents are quite minute in their detail. These documents relate to the supply of clothing firstly to the soldiers in Judaea, and secondly to the armies in Cappadocia. It is known that both provincial garrisons at this period comprised both legionary and auxiliary troops. So it is surprising that the documents do not specify whether the clothing is for legionaries or auxiliaries. It is debatable, therefore, whether any attempt was made to differentiate between citizen and non-citizen soldiers by the wearing of differently coloured tunics. Although Tacitus (*Hist.*, I, 38; III, 47) refers on a number of occasions to distinctive weapons and equipment used by auxiliaries, in contrast he also alludes to a policy of Romanising the allied armies by giving them Roman armour and standards. If both types of soldier received their clothing

OPPOSITE **Detail of the mid-2nd
century Bridgeness distance slab
from the Antonine Wall in
Scotland (item 25 in the text
catalogue).** The scene shows a
military sacrifice carried out by
members of Legio II Augusta, as
indicated by the *vexillum* flag in
the background. Behind the
central figure, dressed in a
toga – possibly the legion's
commander Claudius Charax –
are four other soldiers. On the
left is a man apparently wearing
a *sagum* cloak; the second from
the right wears a *paenula*. Red
paint was discovered on the
body of the figure at the extreme
right, who is also possibly
wearing a paenula.

Apart from *paenula* and *sagum*,
other terms such as *abolla* and
lacerna are used in ancient
literature, but these may simply
have been alternative names for
the same cloaks rather than
completely different designs.
Classical writers were far more
concerned with style than with
minutiae of physical description,
and were trained to avoid
repeating the same words.

from the same supply sources one could conclude that it was likely that both wore the same colour tunics.

On the other hand, Fuentes suggested that locally recruited auxiliaries could have worn their own traditionally coloured regional clothing. For instance, in the early 1st century the Greek historian Strabo (*Georg.*, 3. 3. 7) described how the men in a number of Spanish tribes dressed in black, which may have been reflected in the colour of the tunics of the tribesmen recruited into the Asturian infantry and cavalry units raised from these regions. Almost certainly, before the reforms of Augustus which established the *auxilia* on a professional footing, new recruits would have provided their own clothing, a practice which may or may not have continued for some time afterwards. If there was a designated colour difference between citizen and non-citizen soldiers it is not known how this applied to those citizens who are known to have formed some units of the *auxilia*, or if the cohorts of citizens were distinguished in any way.

The best evidence for the colour of auxiliary tunics are the frescoes from Dura Europos, Luxor and Castellum Dimidi (to be discussed in the forthcoming second part of this study). Frustratingly, these all date from after the Constitutio Antoniniana by which the Emperor Caracalla (AD 211–217) granted Roman citizenship to all free-born inhabitants of the empire, wiping out at a stroke the traditional differences between citizen legionaries and non-citizen auxiliaries.

(22) Tertullian (born c.AD 160/AD 170), *De Corona Militis*, 1.3.

Tertullian describes a soldier being accused of being a Christian because he refuses to wear a military crown. Before trial can commence the accused is stripped of his military insignia including his cloak, sword and sandals, until he is left clad 'only in red'. Of further interest is Tertullian's description of the military boots as *caliga speculatoria*, which suggests that this unfortunate soldier was a member of the emperor's elite cavalry bodyguard, the *Speculatores Augustii* or 'Augustan Scouts'.

(23) Encaustic (wax) portraits, Egypt; 2nd/3rd century AD

Chronologically it is best to introduce here the funerary portraits from the Fayum district of Egypt, as the finest examples date from the Hadrianic-Severan period. Apion, an Egyptian who enlisted in the Imperial fleet and was transferred to Misenum in Italy, wrote to his father telling him that he had sent by way of a friend a little picture of himself – doubtless a portrait similar to those discovered in Egypt itself. This reminds us that even a fairly humble soldier could afford these works of art and that they do not represent solely the officer class.

Hundreds of these paintings have now been uncovered. They are painted in wax on either linen or wooden panels, a technique known as encaustic. During the person's lifetime these portraits were probably displayed around the house, but when they died they were placed over the face of the deceased and incorporated into the funeral bandages wrapped around the body. In view of the above letter it would not be surprising if some of the surviving portraits represented military men; in fact at least six paintings have now been identified as soldiers, and not as members of the Ptolemaic dynasty as previously believed. This identification rests chiefly on the studded red leather sword baldrics that these figures wear. A comparison with tombstones from the early Principate would strongly suggest that those figures with sword belts crossing from their right shoulder to their left side would be centurions, who at this time wore their swords on the left. Most of these men, whether their belts cross to the left or the right side, wear white tunics and blue cloaks; if some of them are centurions then they are not distinguished in any obvious way. One (see page 22) wears a red cloak.

Although the Fayum portraits generally depict only the subject's head and shoulders another portrait, from Deir-el-Medinah near Luxor and dating to the mid-3rd century AD, shows the soldier down to his waist and reveals much of his sword. Like the men in the other portraits he too wears a white tunic, although it can be seen that the sleeves are long; but this man's cloak is red. His sword is worn on his left side, but unfortunately by this date this feature is no longer unique to centurions.

(24) Arrian (c.AD 129–AD 130), *Ars Tactica*, 34. 1.

Describing the spectacular training displays carried out by the Roman cavalry, Arrian mentioned that instead of armour the troopers wore coloured tunics. Arrian calls these tunics 'Cimmerian', and adds that they were shaped like the body armour. He goes on to say that they were either scarlet, blue or a variety of colours. Together with the decorated standards and the yellow horse-hair crests displayed on these occasions, the cavalry would have presented a colourful spectacle, which was obviously what was intended.

What may in fact be one of these cavalry sports tunics may be illustrated on the tombstone of T.Flavius Draccus, who served with the Ala I Flavia Domitiana Britannica MCR. This tombstone retained evidence of its original colouring, but unfortunately the deceased is only represented in a head-and-shoulders format, unlike the full figures depicted elsewhere on cavalry grave stelae. Draccus appears to wear a blue tunic over a scarf, but this could equally be a blue cloak, which would at least be in keeping with many of the portraits from Egypt (see page 33).

(25) Antonine Wall distance slab, Bridgeness, Scotland; c.AD 142

Wild (1968 & 1985) notes that when painted colour survives on tombstones of civilians in north-west Europe their coats, capes, cloaks and scarves are invariably yellow or yellow-orange outlined in red. The traces of red paint on the cloak of a soldier on the Bridgeness distance slab from Scotland dating to the Antonine period (see page 34) could therefore be from a similar outline. The cloak consequently might originally have been yellow or yellow-brown; but in the light of some of the evidence cited above a red cloak may not be out of the question either.

The scene on the slab represents a military sacrifice, *suovetaurilia*, with a senior officer dressed in a toga and three other figures including a *vexiliarius* behind. One of these soldiers has a *paenula* and scarf while the other wears a *sagum*. It was the *sagum* which retained traces of paint, and Fuentes believed that this man was therefore a centurion.

(26) Tombstone, Haghia Triada, Crete; late 2nd/early 3rd century AD

A tombstone of a marine named Sabinianus detached from the Misenum fleet, found in Crete. He wears a *paenula* over a tunic; traces of red paint were found on both the cloak and tunic.

OTHER CLOTHING

The scarf (focale)

Wearing a scarf around the neck is seen by modern re-enactors as obligatory when wearing close-fitting body armour; it protects the neck from chafing, both by all the various types of armour in use during the Roman period, and by the leather thong that fastens the helmet cheek pieces. Unfortunately, as scarves in various sculptures are almost invariably depicted tucked beneath either the armour or clothing, it is uncertain what shape they were originally.

Most re-enactors favour a triangular design as this fits neatly and comfortably beneath the armour. However, some sculptures of civilians feature scarves that appear quite voluminous. Furthermore, a description of the arrest of St Pionius by soldiers of the provincial governor at Smyrna in the 3rd century also implies that scarves could be quite long: it describes how a scarf is put around the neck of the saint and tightened until he almost chokes (*Martyrdom of Pionius*, 15.5). In this account, written in Greek, the scarf is called a *maphorion*.

Fuentes postulated that different units within the army may have been identified by distinctive coloured scarves. One attractive theory of his was that soldiers in legions created from naval units may have retained a blue scarf out of respect for their origins. A white knotted scarf is clearly visible in both an Egyptian funeral portrait and in a mosaic scene from Apamea. This latter scarf is small when compared with the type worn by Apinosus (see page 38), but is very similar to those on Trajan's Column.

Trousers (bracae)

Trousers were considered by Classical writers of the old school as hopelessly barbarian and effeminate. Cicero, for example, referred contemptuously to the '*bracatae nationes*', 'the trouser-clad peoples' (*Epistulae ad Familiares*, IX, 15, 2, 6). Yet once again the pure Roman ideals were to succumb as first the army, and then society in general adopted these garments. Trousers were known in the Classical world as early as the 5th century BC when the Greeks encountered nomadic tribes like the Scythians. Trousers, like boots, were inventions of these warrior horsemen, and it is very likely that it was the Scythians who passed on these fashions to other peoples like the Celts and Germans. The Greeks, however, unlike the Romans, remained true to their principles and never wore trousers.

Two main types of trousers were favoured by the Scythians: the first was close-fitting and made of leather, the second a far looser and wider type made from wool. Both of these types could be tucked into short, soft leather riding boots, and both styles may possibly be observed in use in the Roman Empire.

Other variations may also have found their way into the Imperial armies. A pair of wool twill trousers from Thorsberg in Schleswig-Holstein, Germany, dating to the 3rd century AD were fitted with attached 'feet' like medieval footed hose or a modern baby's romper suit. These fairly tight-fitting trousers appear very similar to those illustrated in the fresco showing members of the Roman garrison of Dura Europos and in the mosaics from Piazza Armerina. A pair of trousers carried by a servant on a Roman fresco from Silistria in Bulgaria are

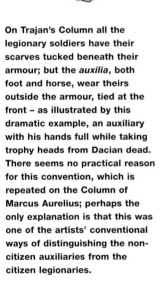

On Trajan's Column all the legionary soldiers have their scarves tucked beneath their armour; but the *auxilia*, both foot and horse, wear theirs outside the armour, tied at the front – as illustrated by this dramatic example, an auxiliary with his hands full while taking trophy heads from Dacian dead. There seems no practical reason for this convention, which is repeated on the Column of Marcus Aurelius; perhaps the only explanation is that this was one of the artists' conventional ways of distinguishing the non-citizen auxiliaries from the citizen legionaries.

again almost identical to those from Thorsberg, and it was probably trousers of this type that the Emperor Honorius tried to ban within the city of Rome as late as AD 397.

While the Gauls are generally represented in Roman sculpture wearing long trousers – e.g. a statuette of a dead warrior found at Alesia – other sculptures also reveal that they wore shorter versions. A figure of a deity now in Dijon Museum, France, wears trousers reaching just below the knee, as does another example in the collection of the Musée des Antiquités Nationales. These are the type of trousers, more commonly referred to as breeches or *bracae*, that are familiar from Trajan's Column. On this monument *bracae* are worn by all the auxiliary soldiers as well as the senior Roman officers, including the Emperor Trajan himself, but not the legionaries. On the contemporary monument known as the Tropaeum Trajani at Adamklissi, however, even the legionary soldiers are seen wearing them.

Their introduction into the Roman army was no doubt via the Celtic, German and Eastern auxiliary troops recruited into the army in increasing numbers from the time of Julius Caesar; it is now accepted that the word bracae itself is Germanic in origin. Trousers would anyway be more practical in northern climates, but it is perhaps not surprising that it is on the tombstones of cavalrymen that they first appear officially as part of the Roman uniform. The Rhineland tombstone of the Thracian trooper T.Flavius Bassus of the Ala Noricorum is a particularly fine example; he also retains his un-Roman long sleeved tunic.

Socks (*udones*)

The very idea that socks were worn during the Roman period was only brought to general attention by their mention in one of the first translated writing tablets from Vindolanda. However, their existence in Roman contexts had long been known from other sources. A close examination of the Cancelleria relief reveals that at least one of the Praetorians was wearing socks that were open at the toes and heels; these are visible between the straps on his leather boots, and were probably a contrasting colour, like those worn by fashionable civilians.

Wearing socks undoubtedly provided a degree of protection from chafing by the leather boots. However, the open design of the early marching boot allowed air to circulate and was free-draining, so that if the feet got wet they would dry quicker if the soldier were not wearing socks. Under normal campaign conditions they would probably be dispensed with.

The waistband (*fascia ventralis*)

A study of grave stelae of the early Empire – specifically those of P.Flavoleius Cordus from Legio XIIII Gemina, and Daverzus from Cohors IIII Delmatarum (see pages 8 and 3) – seems to indicate a waist sash worn underneath the military belt. Pliny the Elder records the existence of waist sashes made from rough wool (*Nat. Hist.*, VIII, lxxiii, 193). The sashes on the tombstones appear identical to those frequently observed worn by figures of the *lares* or household gods. A fresco in the House of the Vettii

The tombstone of Apinosus, a workman from Nievre in France, shows a rare instance of a scarf worn outside the other clothing. This particular example is a long strip of material – estimated at about 1.70m – with fringed ends. It is very similar to two scarves found in an Iron Age burial from Denmark; and, of course, to countless scarves worn today.

BELOW **Barbarian auxiliary from Trajan's Column, wearing baggy trousers; there appears to be a fabric belt around his waist, but it could also be the top of the trousers rolled down. Finds of similar trousers from Germanic sites have added belt-loops around the waist.**

Children's socks from either end of the Roman Empire: top, from Egypt, and above, from Vindolanda, England. They illustrate the varying quality in Roman textiles as well as two different sock designs. The Egyptian version would be worn with open, sandal-type boots and has a separately knitted big toe to allow a boot strap to pass between the toes. The Vindolanda example is crude by comparison, and is made from an upper and sole roughly tacked together; this type could be worn with the enclosed type of boots. (The Manchester Museum, The University of Manchester; and Vindolanda Museum)

A *calceus* – an enclosed boot of the type used by officers – found at the isolated desert fort at Qasr, Ibrim, Egypt. (Copyright The British Museum)

in Pompeii shows two *lares* wearing purple-coloured sashes over their white tunics. A similar colour scheme could be envisaged worn by off-duty military men.

Experiments by Peter de Haas with a reconstructed waistband used a piece of material 350cm long x 30cm wide. A number of observations were made when the waistband was worn with replica armour. It was found that the waistband supported the back, making it easier to endure the weight of the armour. A waistband would also have prevented any rough edges from the rivets on the back of the belts from ripping the tunic; and would certainly cover any tucks around the waist if they were deemed unsightly. If the last turn of the waistband was doubled a pouch about 15cm deep was created, providing a useful pocket. On military tombstones a rectangular object often appears to be tucked into the waistband, and in the case of the *auxilia* this has been referred to as their discharge diplomas. However, as legionaries carry them too, alternative suggestions are that they are writing tablets or leather purses.

If Roman soldiers did indeed adopt the practice of wearing waistbands, then two other sculptures may suggest where they originated. An Etruscan warrior on an urn from Volterra has a band of material wound around his waist instead of a belt; and the sculpture of a Celt now in Avignon Museum, France, also reveals a similar band of material, but in this case just visible beneath his sword belt. In both instances the warriors wear their sashes over a mail shirt, perhaps adding a splash of colour to an armour that was otherwise quite dull.

Military boots

In spite of being perhaps the best-known item of military clothing, there is practically no evidence – archaeological, sculptural or otherwise – for Republican military footwear. Invariably sculptures from this period depict Roman soldiers barefoot, but it is generally accepted among modern scholars that the details of footwear would originally have been added in paint which has long since worn off.

One notable exception is a tombstone from Padua in Italy representing Minucius, a centurion, which appears to show an enclosed boot probably of the type known in the Imperial period as a *calceus*. The *calceus* came in three variants which reflected the status of the wearer – either patrician, senatorial or equestrian. Therefore in the army they would only ever be worn by senior officers, including the emperor if he led his troops in the field. There are references in Roman literature to the boots of senators being either scarlet or black, which could be interpreted as meaning they were made of leather dyed scarlet tied up with black thonged laces. *Calcei* were almost certainly made with soft leather uppers that do not survive very well, while sculptures also show them as having a clearly defined separate sole. Consequently

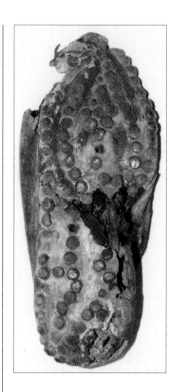

The sole of a badly worn hob-nailed military boot from Vindolanda, England, perhaps evidence of the apparent difficulty of supplying this particular fort situated in the centre of the northern frontier zone. While providing a firm grip on grass the nails on the soles could produce fatal results on an excessively smooth surface: Josephus records the death of a centurion during the Jewish wars, who slipped and fell while leading a charge across the stone-flagged floor of the Antonia fortress in Jerusalem (*BJ*, 6.1.8). Modern re-enactors encounter similar problems with reconstructed boots on many of today's smooth road and pedestrian surfaces. (Vindolanda Museum)

a number of sewn boot soles found on military sites of the 1st century AD have been identified as the remains of *calcei*.

Due to lack of evidence it is impossible to say when the 'classic' military boots, *caligae*, first appeared, but they were certainly in common use by the German campaigns of Augustus and his successor Tiberius. The story of Gaius, the future emperor, is well known but illustrates how closely *caligae* were associated with the military at this date. As a small boy Gaius accompanied his father Germanicus, the adopted son of Tiberius, on campaign in Germany; the child commonly wore miniature versions of the soldier's boots, and was given the nickname 'Little Boots' by which he is infamously known to posterity – Caligula.

This association is further supported by an episode in 'The Satyricon' by Petronius. His hero Encolpius tries to pass himself off as a soldier when he is stopped in the street by a soldier for wearing a sword; the real soldier immediately sees through Encolpius' deception because of the white slippers he is wearing.

Despite their appearance *caligae* are in fact boots rather than sandals. *Caligae* were made from cow or ox leather prepared by a vegetable tanning process which took at least two years to complete. Each boot consisted of three layers: an insole, an outer sole, and an upper, which with its distinctive latticework cut-outs gave the boots their familiar sandal-like look. The layers of the sole were clenched together by iron nails which, when hammered into a boot placed on an anvil or last, recurved into the leather. It has been noted that the sound of thousands of men in nailed boots marching in step on metalled roads would have provided an audible reminder of the power of Rome. Juvenal warns pedestrians about encountering a soldier in the street and getting their toes trodden on by his hob-nailed boots; and advises against provoking soldiers, who might kick their shins in retaliation (*Sat.* iii, 232 & xvi, 25).

The open latticework upper provided excellent ventilation, reducing the possibility of sweaty feet and blisters, as well as being free-draining. In addition the flexible straps could be adjusted to adapt to the wearer's foot. Practical experiments with reconstructions show that abrasions to the feet are minimal because of the absence of pressure on toe joints, the ankle and big toe, but socks could also be worn for additional comfort or in cold weather. The *caligae* were laced together with thongs tied through the openwork strap ends; indeed, the ridge effect caused by this method is often the only feature of the boot which appears on soldiers' tombstones, the other details obviously being added in paint.

Apart from minor variations surviving *caligae* are extremely standardised, suggesting that pattern models were issued for the soldiers themselves to copy, perhaps under the supervision of a unit shoemaker. Except in extreme cases there is little evidence to suggest that boots were constantly repaired, which implies that it was quicker and easier to replace them entirely than to attempt repairs. A document from Egypt records how a soldier was issued with three pairs of boots per year, which gives a rough lifespan for *caligae* that modern experiments with reconstructed examples seem to corroborate. However, the letter to his father from Claudius Terentianus, who was attached to the Alexandrian fleet early in the 2nd century AD, reveals that some boots were clearly unsuitable. He describes a particular style of boot as worthless, states that he has to provide himself with footwear twice in a month, and pleads with his father to send him three new leather boots and some felt socks. (In a further illuminating comment he asks his father to send him a new pickaxe because the one sent previously had been taken by an *optio* – a centurion's second in command).

Long periods of marching also wore out the nails, and during the civil wars of AD 69 troops of the Danubian army demanded 'nail money', *clavarium* (Tac., *Hist.*, 3.50). Similarly, after the wars a detachment of the marine fire brigade who were constantly on the move between Ostia, Puteoli and Rome applied for a special boot allowance, *calciarium*; (Suet., *Vesp.*, 8, 3).

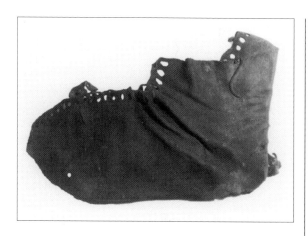

Enclosed marching boot from Vindolanda, England. These were among the early successors to the classic *caligae*. (Vindolanda Museum)

Unfortunately the new emperor Vespasian was renowned for being tight-fisted as well as a strict disciplinarian; he rejected their application, and instead ordered that to prevent wear and tear on their boots in future they should march barefoot...

Although the use of nailed soles continued for some time, it comes as something of a surprise to discover that *caligae* do not appear to have continued in service beyond the 1st century AD. This is illustrated quite dramatically at the late 1st century site of Vindolanda by the complete absence of *caligae* from the archaeological record. The reason is as yet still open to speculation. It might simply reflect some difficulty of supply to this particular site: almost uniquely, it was reported that the boots from this early phase at Vindolanda had been repaired many times, and in some cases had even been worn until all the nails had fallen out and the soles were worn flat. However, later documents from Vindolanda record soldiers buying individual nails for their boots – as few as six in one case, as many as 350 in another. An alternative suggestion is that as the army became more static and settled in permanent bases the manufacture of equipment largely passed into the hands of civilian contractors rather than unit craftsmen on the spot, with consequent uncertainties of delivery.

This is supported by the new style of boot adopted by the army, which rapidly replaced the *caligae*. These boots have enclosed sides and toes which give a more recognisable modern boot-like appearance. Compared with the earlier *caligae* these would be far easier to produce, being no different from the type worn by civilians engaged in heavy duty occupations such as dock workers. From the 2nd century AD, therefore, it is not so easy for archaeologists to identify the presence of soldiers simply by the surviving traces of their boots alone, and even male footwear is often only recognisable from female by size.

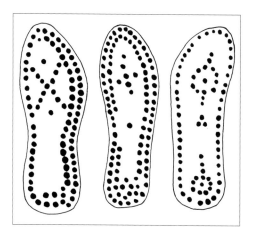

Late 1st century AD nailing patterns from Vindolanda, after C.van Driel-Murray. Nails were not hammered into the sole in a random manner, but in regular patterns which demonstrate that the Romans understood the principles of the distribution of weight on the foot during marching. Weight is placed first on the heel and then transferred forwards diagonally towards the big toe. Accordingly, the placement of the nails generally follows a 'D'-shaped pattern. Modern scholars have noted that the Romans anticipated the principles of computer-designed sport shoes almost 2,000 years earlier.

MISCELLANEOUS ITEMS

On rare occasions we get glimpses of Roman soldiers wearing completely non-military items of dress, at times even when on active service. The most obvious occasions would be when they were carrying out undercover operations when they would be obliged to dress like civilians. One instance of this occurred during the governorship of the notorious Pontius Pilate in Judaea. Forewarned of a potential demonstration against the building of an aqueduct in Jerusalem, Pilate ordered some of his soldiers to dress in local clothes and mingle with the crowd; on a given signal they broke up the demonstration by using clubs concealed beneath their cloaks.

Some tombstones show soldiers off duty. The scenes actually represent a funerary banquet, so the men are depicted reclining on dining couches being attended by a servant. They wear a loose tunic and drape the cloak around their bodies. On other formal occasions, when officers conducted religious services, they would also dress in civilian clothes – usually the *toga*.

As well as the socks, *udones*, which are mentioned on a Vindolanda writing tablet, the same document records the gift of two pairs of underpants, *subligariorum*. This draft letter reminds us that soldiers were able to receive items of clothing from home, although whether they could wear them on duty is uncertain. The Vindolanda documents also record other items of clothing, though the exact nature of many must for the time being remain speculative. They include undertunics, *subuclas*; undercloaks, *subpaenulas*; overcoats, *superarias*; and even cloaks made from bark, *sagacorticia*. The latter is not as absurd as it sounds, as it probably means the bast fibres on the inside of bark – this material had been used for making garments since Neolithic times, but was probably regarded by the Romans as a bit primitive. The so-called 'hairmoss' cap from Vindolanda might also fall into this category; it has actually been suggested that this was the remains of a Roman wig, but the best guess is that it is in fact a cap – and one with very ancient ancestors.

Garments evidently had new uses even after they were worn out; for instance, cloaks were frequently used as burial shrouds. There also appears to have been a thriving second-hand clothes industry which cut up old garments into squares and made new items from them. Cato suggested that this should be done with old tunics when new ones were issued to farm workers (*de Agri.*, LIX). This practice was highlighted by the recent discovery of a partially complete tunic at the Imperial quarries at Mons Claudianus in Egypt (see page 43). This appeared to have been manufactured from the remains of an old cloak, as there were distinctive 'gamma' patterns – which are normally found in the corners of cloaks – positioned haphazardly on the tunic. Old clothes could also be cut up and put to other uses, such as packing for pottery or other valuable items. Soldiers undoubtedly cleaned armour and equipment with old rags, while other pieces could be made into leggings. Less glamorous, perhaps, were the pieces of clothing that ultimately ended their days as 'toilet paper'; nevertheless it is generally in these fragmentary states that the textiles themselves are preserved to be discovered by archaeologists.

Detail of a relief in Rome showing a sacrificial scene from the time of Marcus Aurelius. The attendant is dressed exactly as similar military attendants are shown on Trajan's Column.

BIBLIOGRAPHY

Antonucci, C., *L'Esercito di' Cesare 54–44 a.c.*, (Milan, 1996)

Becatti, G., *The Art of Ancient Greece and Rome*, (London, 1968)

Bishop, M.C., *The Development of Roman Military Equipment in the First Century AD and its relevance to the Army and Society*, (Sheffield, 1981)

Bishop, M.C., & Coulston, J.C.N., *Roman Military Equipment*, (London, 1993)

Cotton, D.L., & Geiger, J., *Masada II: Final Report, The Latin and Greek Documents*, (Jerusalem, 1989)

Doxiadis, E., *The Mysterious Fayum Portraits: Faces from Roman Egypt*, (London, 1995)

Fink, R.O., *Roman Military Records on Papyrus*, (Case Western Reserve University, 1971)

Fuentes, N., 'The Roman Military Tunic', in Dawson (ed.), *Roman Military Equipment: The Accoutrements of War, Proceedings of the Third Military Equipment Research Seminar, British Archaeological Report*, Int Ser 336, 1987 (Oxford)

Meyboom, P.G.P., *The Nile Mosaic of Palestrina*, (New York, 1995)

Sebesta, J., & Bonfante, L. (eds.), *The World of Roman Costume*, (Wisconsin, 1994)

Sekunda, N., *The Ptolemaic Army*, (Stockport, 1995)

Shaw, T., 'Roman Cloaks', *Exercitus, 1, 4* and *5*, 1982 (Gloucester)

Sheffer, A., & Granger-Taylor, H., *Masada IV: Final Report, The Textiles*, (Jerusalem, 1994)

Sumner, G., *Roman Army: Wars of the Empire*, (London, 1997)

Wild, J.P., 'The Clothing of Britannia, Gallia Belgica and Germania Inferior', *ANRW, Teil II, p.362–423*, 1985

Principal ancient sources (available as either Loeb Classical Library or Penguin translations):

Appian, *Civil Wars; The Augustan Histories* (Scriptores Historiae Augustae – SHA); Caesar, *The Civil War* and *The Gallic War;* Dio Cassius, *History;* Frontinus, *Strategems;* Horace, *Satires;* Isidorus, *Origins;* Juvenal, *The Sixteen Satires;* Livy, *The History of Rome;* Martial, *Epigrams;* Ovid, *Ars Amatoria;* Petronius, *Satyricon;* Plautus, *Miles Gloriosus;* Pliny the Elder, *Natural History;* Plutarch, *Lives;* Suetonius, *Lives of the Twelve Caesars;* Tacitus, *Annals* and *Histories;* Varro, *On Agriculture*, and *Latin Language;* Vegetius, *Epitome of Military Science;* Virgil, *The Aeneid*.

Tombstone of a cavalryman, M.Aemilius Durises from Cologne, Germany. The deceased is shown as if at his funerary banquet dressed in civilian clothing, along with his servant.

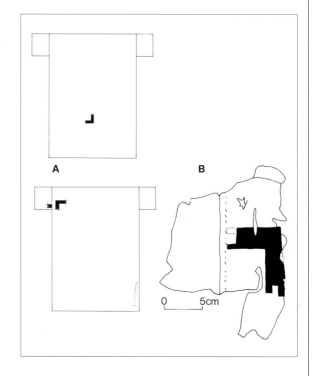

Examples of recycled clothing – not to scale. (A) Both sides of a tunic made up from an old cloak, found at Mons Claudianus, Egypt (after Mannering). (B) Textile fragment with a 'gamma' pattern found at Vindolanda, England (after Wild); the gamma was a darker colour, probably purple, and was almost certainly from a cloak. Like the example from Egypt, this fragment appears to have come from a garment made up from re-used cloth.

THE PLATES

A: THE FALL OF THE REPUBLIC

A1: Gaius Julius Caesar, c.57 BC

Almost everything Caesar did was calculated to get himself noticed, and this naturally extended to his taste in dress. Apart from his famous red cloak there is little mention of distinctive military equipment; but Suetonius tells us that on at least one occasion during the Gallic war, Caesar dressed as a Gaul to pass through enemy territory (*Suet.*, LVIII). In the battle against the Nervii (57 BC) Caesar grabbed a legionary shield and fought in the front rank to encourage his men. Here the shield is based on an example shown on stone reliefs from Narbonne, France, probably from a monument commemorating the conquest of Gaul. It is decorated with gold- and silver-plated fittings as described by Suetonius (Suet., LXVII). Caesar's muscle cuirass is also based on the Narbonne reliefs. Although it is decorated with a lozenge or rhomboid motif it is rather plain by comparison with other statues showing armoured figures, and the reliefs may therefore accurately record Caesar's battle armour.

A2: Marcus Licinius Crassus, c.53 BC

Although Crassus earned a reputation for amassing a vast fortune by highly unscrupulous methods, his career was not without military success, his most notable exploit being the defeat of Spartacus in 71 BC. It was his desire to emulate the achievements of Caesar and Pompey the Great that led to his death at Carrhae during a disastrous campaign against the Parthians. Crassus is depicted here as described by Plutarch, 'replacing his black cloak with a purple one' (*Plu.*, XXIII). His portrait is copied from a bust in the Louvre, Paris, but amended to match Cicero's description of Crassus as the 'bald heir of the Nannei'.

A3: Sextus Pompeius (died c.36 BC)

Although represented by Augustan propaganda as little more than a pirate, Pompeius was in fact one of Rome's few successful admirals. He established an independent power base in Sicily, and remained a thorn in the side of the second Triumvirate until his defeat in 36 BC. As a result of

his long run of victories at sea Pompeius styled himself 'Son of Neptune' and wore a blue cloak, according to both Appian and Dio Cassius (XLVIII, 48). It was unusual for Romans of this period to wear beards but Pompeius clearly wears one on his coins, perhaps in mourning for his father Pompey the Great.

All three men were both patricians and senators and thus entitled to a *paludamentum* cloak and a tunic with broad purple stripes – the *tunica laticlavia*. All three wear the distinctive *calcei* boots worn by Rome's elite; various versions of these are indicated in Roman literature and art. Caesar wore red-coloured boots (*Dio Cassius*, XLIII), while others could be tied with black thongs or decorated with silver crescents (*Juvenal*, VII, 192).

B: GUARDIANS OF THE NORTH

B1: Legionary, Germany, AD 14

At the beginning of the reign of Tiberius the armies on the Rhine and Danube frontiers mutinied over service conditions. The physical appearance of this legionary matches the account by Tacitus, while his armour and equipment are based as closely as possible on the latest discoveries from Kalkriese, acknowledged as one of the sites of the running battle known as the 'Varus disaster' in AD 9. He is wearing a red military tunic and has replaced the standard issue boots with a type called *carbatinae*, which are frequently found on military sites in Britain and Germany, but are not normally considered military boots. He has adopted a native fashion – around his legs are wool wrappings, which sculptural evidence from this period would suggest was certainly not an official practice. The shield, based on the Arch of Orange, France, shows a design associated with

Legio II Augusta, who were involved in the mutinies and were later based in Britain.

B2: Auxiliary, Germany, AD 20–50
Reconstruction of a dress uniform for an auxiliary infantryman based on Rhineland tombstones, in particular that of Annaius Daverzus from Cohors IIII Delmatarum (see page 3). Without evidence from the inscriptions on these tombstones there is often no obvious way of telling whether the soldier is a legionary or an auxiliary – in fact the auxiliary tombstones are sometimes more elaborate than their legionary counterparts. As neither tunics nor cloaks had pockets, valuables could be tucked into the waistband, and many tombstones appear to show a purse protruding from its folds.

B3: *Beneficiarius*, Britain, AD 70
This figure is based on the tombstone found at Camomile Street, London, which almost certainly represents one of the provincial governor's staff. The soldier was possibly a *beneficiarius*, a man selected to carry out wide-ranging specialist administrative duties, indicated by the wax-coated writing tablets which he carries. These duties included intelligence, internal security and supervision of tax-collecting. Both legionaries and auxiliaries held this rank, and again there is no known distinction, perhaps other than quality of equipment. *Beneficiarii* were identified by a special lancehead; this example is from Germany – later versions became very elaborate. He wears a white (unbleached) *paenula*, as described in a document from Vindolanda on Hadrian's Wall, and enclosed boots with socks based on finds from the same site.

C: OUTPOSTS OF EMPIRE

C1: Auxiliary, Caesarea, Algeria, AD 40
Unlike the tombstones of similar date from the Rhineland,

those from modern-day Algeria reveal a simple style of tunic and cloak. Black *clavi* are seen in several North African sources but their use at this period is conjectural. Like many cosmopolitan centres in the empire Caesarea had a volatile population and riots were common. This figure is probably in walking-out-dress, and a cudgel known as a *fustis* was a necessary addition. They were used in crowd control – and to beat to death soldiers who fell asleep on sentry duty, a punishment known as *fustuarium*.

C2: Auxiliary, Judaea c.AD 30
This soldier is dressed in local garb, which follows Greek fashions, while carrying out surveillance duties. A truncheon is concealed beneath his cloak (known in the Greek-speaking East as a *himation*); although not visible from this angle, the corners would probably be decorated with 'gamma'-shaped designs in contrasting colour – see Plate H3. Jewish sandals appear to have been worn without characteristic Roman hobnails (*Shabbat* 6.2). One modern explanation for this was that nailed boots enabled Jews to hear when Roman soldiers were approaching...

C3: Auxiliary centurion, Judaea, c.AD 30
This centurion is dressed in a tunic, *paludamentum* and waistband. He holds a *vitis* vine stick, the centurion's notorious badge of rank; it is held in a manner quite different from the way ordinary soldiers hold the *fustis*. According to the Gospels, one of the auxiliary units stationed in Judaea was an 'Italian' cohort; details of costume and equipment are therefore based on finds from Italy, including the waistband from the Cassaco sculpture. However, the sword scabbard is from Pula, Croatia. The Roman soldiers at the crucifixion of Christ divided his clothes amongst themselves by casting lots (*Matthew*, 28, 35–36); if nothing else, this tells us that they had a use for civilian garments.

LEFT **Marching soldier from the Adamklissi monument, Romania, early 2nd century AD – see Plate D1. Unlike his contemporaries depicted on Trajan's Column in Rome he wears no armour and does not carry a marching pack; this may therefore indicate some form of parade or drill dress. Also unlike his fellow legionaries on the Column, he is shown wearing calf-length breeches.**

ABOVE **Two unarmoured soldiers from Trajan's Column – a slinger and a stone-thrower. Both men use their cloaks to carry missiles, and wear similar tunics to the legionaries shown on the Column – cf Plate E3.**

D: EXPANDING THE EMPIRE

D1: Legionary, Dacian Wars, late 1st century AD

Based on the Adamklissi monument in Romania, this marching legionary wears no armour and has no marching pack – unlike his contemporaries depicted on Trajan's Column; this could represent a light marching order or even drill dress. Another difference from Trajan's Column is the use of wool *bracae*, breeches worn to just below the knee. This manner of carrying the *pilum*, like the modern 'slope arms' position, is seen on both the Adamklissi monument and the Cancelleria relief in Rome.

D2 & D3: Legionaries, fatigue dress, Dacian wars

Both men wear the light 'working order' as depicted on Trajan's Column. The rear view **D2** shows the tunic gathered and tied into a knot at the back of the neck. Both men carry the standard army pickaxe or *dolabra*. Trajan's Column still shows all soldiers wearing *caligae*. Figure **D3** is a German recruited into Imperial service. As well as the basic Roman tunic, worn untied and off the right shoulder to allow free movement of the arm, he has retained items of native origin including the knee-length *bracae* and leggings; the design of the latter is based on finds from Denmark, but in this case they have been made from re-cycled tunic cloth.

E: EXPANDING THE EMPIRE

E1, 2 & 3: Auxiliaries, 1st–2nd centuries AD

These are based on the columns of Trajan and Marcus Aurelius. **E2** is a barbarian club-man, probably of German origin, carrying a simple shield made from planks of wood glued together (later even Roman shields would be made in this way). He wears baggy wool trousers similar to those found at Thorsberg, Germany. The short hair is not necessarily indicative of service in the Roman army; Tacitus informs us that it was a custom amongst some Germans to shave off their beards and cut their hair after they had slain an enemy (*Germania*, 31). **E1** is a irregular archer with a long-sleeved tunic, trousers and wool cap; leg bindings – like 19th/20th century puttees – were common in the later Roman period,

but the existence of bandage-like material at the 1st century British site of Vindolanda suggests that they were used even earlier. **E3** is a stone-thrower, perhaps from northern Greece, as troops of this type known as *psiloi* had fought in ancient Greek armies. He uses a 'bagged' fold of his cloak to hold a supply of ammunition.

F: THE POWER BEHIND THE THRONE

1, 2 & 3: Praetorian Guards, 1st–2nd centuries AD

We can only guess at how the personal whims of profligate rulers like Nero (AD 54–68) or Elagabalus (AD 218–222) were reflected in the dress and equipment of the Imperial guards. Figure **F1** may offer a clue, but the evidence is slight and is based on a single wall painting in the Golden House of Nero. He wears a silvered and gilded bronze '*lorica segmentata*' of Corbridge type, but with bronze edging. Together with the Etrusco-Corinthian style of helmet, it gives an overall Hellenistic effect which would be in keeping with the tastes of many emperors, including Hadrian. Around his body is draped a red *paludamentum*.

Figure **F2** is taken from a tavern sign in Pompeii dating before the eruption of Vesuvius in AD 79. The cloak is the common yellow-brown colour but with dark reddish-brown *clavi*. The shield is of traditional design and is based on the near-contemporary Cancellaria relief in Rome; a figure on this relief is dressed in similar fashion to the Pompeii figure, but his cloak is shorter. The men in both sources hold weighted *pila*.

Figure **F3** is a soldier from the Hadrianic relief now in Chatsworth House, England. He wears a loose-fitting tunic over an under-tunic, gathered and tied behind the neck. A studded strap crosses the body from left shoulder to right side at a high angle; it resembles some seen in the later encaustic funerary portraits from Egypt.

G: POLICING THE GREEK EAST

G1: Marine, Athens, mid-2nd century AD

This reconstruction is based on a well preserved tombstone

LEFT **Detail of a fresco from the Golden House, Rome, dating from the time of Nero (AD 54–68). The figure is armoured and equipped in Greek style but seems to wear a Roman '*lorica segmentata*', perhaps indicating that the figure was modelled on a Roman soldier or even a Praetorian Guardsman. His tunic and helmet crest are green, and the cloak – worn like a *paludamentum* – is red. See Plate F1.**

RIGHT **This soldier, probably a Praetorian, is one of a similar group from a relief dating to the reign of Hadrian (AD 117–138) now in Chatsworth House, England – see Plate F3. He wears a loose-fitting tunic tied behind the neck in a knot, with the edge of an under-tunic visible at the hem. In this group several men have a narrow strap over the left shoulder and under the right arm; it is clearly not a sword baldric, and it has been suggested that its purpose was to keep the voluminous folds of the tunic out of the way of the sword hilt.**

found in Greece. Note that the *sagum* has a small tassel on the bottom corner. On the monument the sword appears to be fastened to a fabric belt similar to those normally seen on muscle-cuirassed statues. The use of red for both cloak and tunic is attested by the tombstone of another marine, Sabinianus, found in Crete. The lantern is based on archaeological finds from Pompeii, and is also seen on ships depicted on Trajan's Column.

G2: Centurion, Alexandria, c.AD 150
This figure is largely based on an encaustic portrait found in Egypt. He has a white tunic with black *clavi*, and wears a blue *paludamentum* brooched on the left shoulder. On his head is a gold-plated tin wreath based on an example found in Egypt; a number of portraits show both civilians and military men wearing these crowns, which may therefore indicate prowess on the athletics track rather than the battlefield.

G3: *Diogmitoi*, Ephesos, 2nd century
This policeman is taken from a relief of a senior police officer – called in Greek a *paraphylax* – found near Ephesos in Turkey. This man appears to be greeting his commander, and on the relief he is accompanied by two other men identically equipped. The green cloak – the colour taken from a contemporary Egyptian encaustic portrait – is worn like a *paludamentum*, so he could be of centurial rank. Around the waist is what appears to be an extremely wide waistband, but this reconstruction follows the Italian historian Antonucci, who suggests that it is actually the cloak wrapped around the waist.

H: SERVANTS OF ROME
H1: Legionary under punishment, 1st–2nd century AD
A minor punishment prescribed by Augustus was recorded by Suetonius: 'He would order men to stand all day in front of the general's headquarters, sometimes clad only in their tunics and without sword belts, or sometimes holding a ten-foot pole or even a clod of earth' (*Augustus*, 24.2). The ten-foot pole would be a surveyor's *decempeda* used for measuring, and turfs were the basic material for camp ramparts, which might suggest that this particular punishment was for sloppy work during surveying or construction duties. The humiliation seems to have lain in the removal of the weapon belt – *cingula militaris* – which was particularly associated with military status.

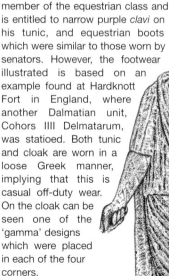

This tombstone from Athens shows a marine wearing a *sagum* cloak with a small tassel visible on one edge – see Plate G1.

A police official salutes his commander in this detail from a relief found near Ephesos in Turkey – see Plate G3. Note the fabric wrapped around his waist. These paramilitary police were known in the Greek-speaking eastern part of the empire as *diogmitoi*.

H2: Senior tribune, 2nd century AD
Tribunes at this period were drawn from the senatorial class, so were distinguished by the broad purple stripe on their tunics, and red senatorial or patrician boots. In this case the tribune is carrying out a sacrifice and wears a *toga*, with a fold worn over his head as a mark of respect for the deity that he invokes – in this case, the 'luck' of the unit.

H3: Commander of auxiliary cohort, 1st–2nd century AD
Inspired by the tombstone of T.Claudius Halotus, commander of a Dalmatian cohort, this officer is a member of the equestrian class and is entitled to narrow purple *clavi* on his tunic, and equestrian boots which were similar to those worn by senators. However, the footwear illustrated is based on an example found at Hardknott Fort in England, where another Dalmatian unit, Cohors IIII Delmatarum, was statioed. Both tunic and cloak are worn in a loose Greek manner, implying that this is casual off-duty wear. On the cloak can be seen one of the 'gamma' designs which were placed in each of the four corners.

Tombstone of T.Claudius Halotus from Cologne, Germany. This commander of a Dalmatian auxiliary cohort evidently chose to be represented in civilian garb rather then military dress for his funeral portrait – see Plate H3.

INDEX

Figures in **bold** refer to illustrations

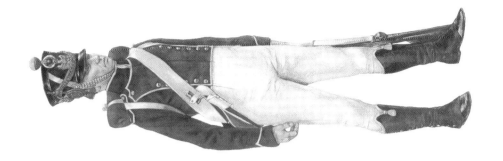

PUBLISHING

FIND OUT MORE ABOUT OSPREY

❏ Please send me the latest listing of Osprey's publications

❏ I would like to subscribe to Osprey's e-mail newsletter

Title/rank

Name

Address

Postcode/zip   state/country

e-mail

I am interested in:

❏ Ancient world   ❏ American Civil War
❏ Medieval world   ❏ World War I
❏ 16th century   ❏ World War II
❏ 17th century   ❏ Modern warfare
❏ 18th century   ❏ Military aviation
❏ Napoleonic   ❏ Naval warfare
❏ 19th century

Please send to:

USA & Canada:
Osprey Direct USA, c/o MBI Publishing, P.O. Box 1,
729 Prospect Avenue, Osceola, WI 54020

UK, Europe and rest of world:
Osprey Direct UK, P.O. Box 140, Wellingborough,
Northants, NN8 2FA, United Kingdom

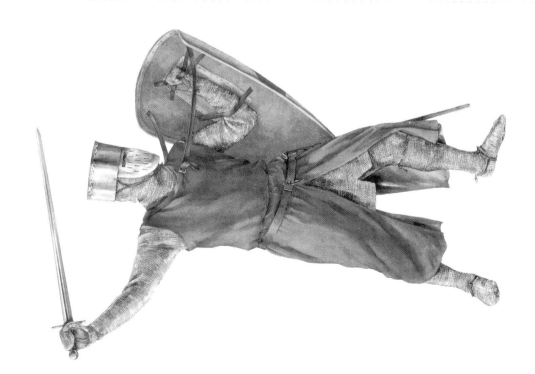

OSPREY
PUBLISHING

www.ospreypublishing.com

call our telephone hotline
for a free information pack

USA & Canada: 1-800-826-6600
UK, Europe and rest of world call:
+44 (0) 1933 443 863

Young Guardsman
Figure taken from *Warrior 22:*
Imperial Guardsman 1799–1815
Published by Osprey
Illustrated by Richard Hook

Knight, c.1190
Figure taken from *Warrior 1: Norman Knight 950 – 1204 AD*
Published by Osprey
Illustrated by Christa Hook

POSTCARD